A LENTEN JOURNEY
with Jesus Christ and
SAINT BENEDICT

An Invitation of Grace,

a Prayer of Hope,

and a Gift of Peace.

A LENTEN JOURNEY
with Jesus Christ and
SAINT BENEDICT

Daily Gospel Readings

with

Selections from the Rule of Saint Benedict

REFLECTIONS AND PRAYERS
BY
REV. JOHN R. FORTIN, O.S.B.

WITH ADDITIONAL INTRODUCTORY MATERIAL BY
SUSAN E. BOND AND PETER J. MONGEAU

Christus
Publishing, LLC

WELLESLEY, MA
www.ChristusPublishing.com

Christus Publishing, LLC
Wellesley, Massachusetts
www.ChristusPublishing.com

Rev. John R. Fortin, O.S.B., has been a Benedictine monk at Saint Anselm Abbey in Manchester, NH since 1970. He was ordained to the priesthood in 1976. He earned graduate degrees from St. John's College (Santa Fe, NM) and from the Medieval Institute at the University of Notre Dame. He is currently a professor in the Philosophy Department at Saint Anselm College.

Susan E. Bond holds a B.A.L.S. in Religious Studies from Georgetown University and an M.A.T.S. in Hebrew Bible and New Testament from Claremont School of Theology. She is an adjunct professor of Religious Studies at George Mason University.

Peter J. Mongeau is the Founder and Publisher of Christus Publishing, LLC.

Publisher's Cataloging-in-Publication Data
Fortin, John R., 1949-
    A Lenten Journey with Jesus Christ and Saint Benedict : daily Gospel readings with selections from the Rule of Saint Benedict : reflections and prayers / by John R. Fortin ; with additional introductory material by Susan E. Bond and Peter J. Mongeau.
    p. ; cm.

    Includes bibliographical references.
    ISBN: 978-0-9841707-0-8

1. Lent--Prayers and devotions. 2. Catholic Church--Prayers and devotions. 3. Benedict, Saint, Abbot of Monte Cassino. 4. Benedictines--History. I. Benedict, Saint, Abbot of Monte Cassino. Regula. II. Bond Susan E. III. Mongeau Peter J. III. Title.

BX2170.L4 F67 2009
242/.34   2009937731

Printed and bound in the United State of America

10   9   8   7   6   5   4   3   2   1

Text design and layout by Peri Swan
This book was typeset in Garamond Premier Pro with Snell Roundhand as a display typeface

CONTENTS

ACKNOWLEDGMENTS

The Gospel passages are taken from the *Lectionary for Mass for Use in the Dioceses of the United States of America, second typical edition* © 2001, 1998, 1997, 1986, 1970, Confraternity of Christian Doctrine, Inc., Washington, DC. Used with permission. All rights reserved. No portion of this text may be reproduced by any means without permission in writing from the copyright owner.

The citations from the Rule of Saint Benedict are from Terrence Kardong, *Benedict's Rule: A Translation and Commentary.* Copyright by The Order of Saint Benedict, Inc. Published by The Liturgical Press, Collegeville, MN. Reprinted with permission.

Reflections and prayers copyright © 2009 Christus Publishing, LLC.

AN INVITATION
FROM
SAINT BENEDICT

"Listen, O my son, to the teachings of your master, and turn to them with the ear of your heart."

With these words, Saint Benedict opens the Prologue of his Rule for monasteries. They are words that are not addressed to a general audience, but to a specific individual (hence the use of the singular in the Latin) who is inclined to consider entering the monastic life. Later in the Rule, Saint Benedict will speak more directly to the manner in which a candidate would become part of the community, and he will emphasize once again the importance of an attentive listening to the words of wisdom that come from the Scriptures, from the revered masters of monastic doctrine, and even from the very people with whom the candidate wishes to live as a monk.

But the opening words of the Prologue are addressed not only to an aspirant to the cloister. They are also addressed to anyone who wishes to examine and adapt the spirituality of the Rule of Saint Benedict, a spirituality that has been followed and esteemed through fifteen centuries by monastics and lay people alike (see appendix A).

This book, *A Lenten Journey with Jesus Christ and Saint Benedict*, is an invitation to you to listen to the teachings of one of the great spiritual masters of the Catholic Church and to turn the ear of your heart to his wisdom as he shows the way to Christ and calls us to walk in that way, indeed, to run in it: "As we progress . . . our hearts will swell with the unspeakable sweetness of love, enabling us to race along the way of God's commandments."

Listen, then, O reader, and come to know the spiritual depths of Saint Benedict, a man who thought that there was nothing more important in life than to seek God and for whom nothing was to be preferred to the love of Christ. Benedict found God in many different ways: in the goodness and wonders of creation; in his fellow human beings, created in the image and likeness of God; in the prayerful reading of the Scriptures; in the Sacraments and in the prayer of the Church. This book can help you to journey with Jesus and Saint Benedict in Lent and thus help you to seek God more fervently and to live according to his commandments in faith, hope, and love.

REV. JOHN R. FORTIN, O.S.B.

SAINT BENEDICT:
A SHORT
BIOGRAPHY

Just as we do, Saint Benedict lived in interesting times (c. 480–c. 547), yet by the example of his life and in his Rule, this humble and unworldly man made extraordinary contributions to the conversion of Europe and its consequent economic and educational flourishing. In fact, it is only a small understatement to say that the history of western Christianity in the medieval era can be learned by tracking the impact of the Rule of Saint Benedict on the monasteries, cathedrals, and castles of western Europe.

But this unassuming man did not set out to accomplish great things, rather he set out to seek God in a worldly, status-conscious age not unlike our own, by first living as a solitary monk in the regions outside Rome, then taking on the responsibility of founding twelve small monastic houses, and finally becoming the abbot of his most famous monastery, Monte Cassino. Most likely, it is here, from his wise understanding of human nature and his constant effort to protect the weak and direct the strong, that Saint Benedict wrote his Rule, which was to become the primary Rule for the West. To understand the life of Benedict, we begin by putting his life into the context of his times with the Roman Empire, the Church, and monasticism.

THE ROMAN EMPIRE

At the time of Saint Benedict's birth, the western part of the Roman Empire was going into a fatal decline; the city of Rome was sacked in 410 for the first time, shaking the confidence of late antiquity in her invincibility. In 476, only four years before Benedict's birth, the last western Roman emperor, Romulus Augustulus, was deposed by the Germanic refugee Odovacar. Nonetheless, Rome was the political power of the age and although the Roman world was fast becoming a Christian empire, the old classical educational system and its pagan political ideologies were a powerful force in Saint Benedict's world.

THE CHURCH

Christianity came into its own in the fourth century, about a century and a half before Benedict, after Constantine's victory at the Milvian Bridge and the Edict of Milan in 313, which made Christianity a legal religion rather than a persecuted minority. In Benedict's time, the center of the Christian world was shifting toward the East and Constantinople even as the western Church remained an important force for stability in the West. Some of the greatest Doctors of the Church like Saint Augustine of Hippo and Saint Jerome, translator of the Bible into Latin, lived and worked less than a century before Saint Benedict.

MONASTICISM

Monasticism has always been important to the life of the Church, contributing to it a deepened spiritual focus as well as great leaders. Beginning with Saint Anthony of Egypt in the third century, who lived as a solitary in the Egyptian desert practicing great austerities, many were inspired to follow the monastic way and soon the deserts and remote places of Egypt, Syria, Palestine, and Asia Minor were dotted with monastic communities. Most monks lived in community but the monastic ideal was to live an ascetic, if not hermetic life, to vanquish the ways of the devil in one's life. Another early trend was the practice of wealthy Roman Christians opening up their estates for monastic retreats and hospitals. Monastics like Pachomius, Basil, and John Cassian wrote Rules for these various communities.

LIFE OF SAINT BENEDICT

What we know of Saint Benedict comes from Saint Gregory the Great's (Pope Gregory I, 590–604) *Dialogues of Saint Gregory* (see Suggestions for Further Reading), written about fifty years after Saint Benedict's death. Saint Gregory based his story on the accounts of Benedict's disciples, Constantinus, the Abbot of Monte Cassino after Saint Benedict, and Honoratus, Abbot of Subiaco.

Saint Gregory begins his account of Saint Benedict: "There was a man of venerable life, blessed by grace, and blessed in name, for he was called *Benedictus* or Benedict: who, from his younger years carried always the mind of an old man" (*Dialogues of Gregory*, Jolly 1997, 136). In other words, Benedict was wise beyond his years. This is our first view of him and the evidence of his life bears out this interesting observation.

Benedict was born in Nursia to a noble Roman family; as a young man, he went to Rome to pursue his education in classical literary studies. Like a college degree today, a literary education was the path to success for the upper-class person of the era. Perhaps because the empire was in decline, Benedict found the life of his companions in Rome to be dissolute and soon he abandoned this course to seek God: "forsaking his father's house and wealth, with a resolute mind only to serve God" (ibid.). Saint Benedict fled Rome, at first with his childhood nurse, who tenderly loved him, and then to a cave by a fountain and a lake near Subiaco about fifty miles outside Rome, where he was tended by a monk named Romanus from a nearby monastery. Saint Benedict lived there for three years.

Saint Gregory recalls a host of miracles Saint Benedict performed in this period, most of them simple miracles to help working people: blessing a heavy stone that could not be lifted and then lifts with ease, mending a broken sieve, and discerning the prideful thoughts of a monk. The stories give us a picture of a loving person, involved in the day-to-day contretemps of life, yet also a perceptive man, wise to the ways of the human heart.

The story continues when the nearby monks ask Benedict to become their abbot but their hearts are unfaithful and soon they plot to kill Saint Benedict! The saint left to found twelve monasteries of twelve monks each, which he tended until he and some of his monks went to Monte Cassino eighty miles south to found a monastery there. In this story, we see the picture of a man seeking God, in communion with others on the same path, some good and some not so good—perhaps it is these experiences that gave Saint Benedict the impetus to write his Rule.

THE RULE OF SAINT BENEDICT

The Rule of Saint Benedict is a framework for the measured formation of character that aims to transfigure the monk and his community with the help of the Holy Spirit and through the love of Christ. Benedict calls the Rule "a school for the Lord's service" (Prol 45). The effort is to patiently conform the will to God through the steady work of humble service and a day ordered by prayer, rather than by self-punishment or dramatic austerities that Benedict might have called "too much drama."

The Benedictine vows are stability (to remain in one monastery for life), conversion of life (to be faithful to monastic life), and obedience. These vows guide those seeking God to live in community, pray, read Scripture, and work together, that is, to form one mind in service to God. The Benedictine Rule also promotes learning, hospitality, and humility, and expects a lifelong commitment to the monastic community.

Saint Benedict's time was chaotic and uncertain, so the Benedictine community was a place of stability and serenity in "interesting times."

The ideal for monks was asceticism, but Saint Benedict's Rule provides a day ordered by prayer, work, and the reading of Scripture, rather than by extreme adversity. Saint Benedict's era was marked by competition for status, which thrives on the sin of pride, so Saint Benedict's Rule asks for obedience, the counterweight to pride. As the Rule of Benedict spread throughout Europe via Charlemagne and others, Benedictine values ennobled work and promoted a disciplined life, which made Benedictine houses the engine of Europe's economic rise in the medieval era. The Bendictine focus on study and reading Scripture made the Benedictine monasteries centers of learning in Europe. The organizational values of pastoral care and obedience made Benedictine monasteries an example of successful working communities, providing a much-needed stable infrastructure for European life.

DEATH AND SAINT SCHOLASTICA

Saint Benedict lived out his remaining years as abbot and spiritual master of Monte Cassino. Benedict died there between 543 and 547 and is buried there next to his sister, Saint Scholastica, who founded a community of women religious who followed her brother's Rule.

THE ABBEY OF MONTE CASSINO

The Lombards, Saracens, Napoleon, and most recently, the Allies in World War II, sacked, bombed, or destroyed the ancient Abbey of Monte Cassino; each time the abbey was rebuilt.

Sources: Peter Brown, *The Rise of Western Christendom,* 2nd ed. (Malden, MA: Blackwell, 2003); Esther de Waal, *Seeking God: The Way of Saint Benedict,* (Collegeville, MN: The Liturgical Press, 2001); Hugh Ford, "Saint Benedict of Nursia," in *The Catholic Encyclopedia* (New York: Robert Appleton, 1907) available at New Advent http://www.newadvent.org/cathen (accessed August 8, 2009); Karen Louise Jolly, "The Dialogues of Saint Gregory Book II: The Life of Saint Benedict" in *Tradition & Diversity: Christianity in a World Context to 1500* (Armonk, NY: M.E. Sharpe, 1997); Howard Clark Kee, et al., eds., *Christianity: A Social and Cutural History,* 2nd ed. (Upper Saddle River, NJ, 1998); the Web site of The Order of Saint Benedict available at www.osb.org (accessed August 8, 2009).

The Rule of Saint Benedict, however, has never been destroyed—it lives on in faithful Christians like yourself who take up the daily task of ordering the will to God, with the help of the Holy Spirit and through the love of Jesus Christ.

SUSAN E. BOND

THE ORDER OF SAINT BENEDICT: A BRIEF HISTORY

Saint Benedict established the Abbey at Monte Cassino in the year 529 but did not formally establish an order. The Order of Saint Benedict (O.S.B.) is a congregation of independent monastic houses that observe the Rule of Saint Benedict. The Benedictines are known as the "black monks" because of their characteristic black robes.

The Abbey of Monte Cassino was destroyed by the Lombards only forty years after Saint Benedict's death and the monks fled to Rome where they were given refuge at a monastery next to the Lateran Basilica where they stayed for one hundred and forty years, which had the salubrious effect of making their Rule known to the wider world.

THE DAY: ORDERING TIME

The central practice of the Order of Saint Benedict is ordering the day by the life of common prayer; there are seven prayer times during the day and one at night. The prayers are Matins at daybreak, Prime, Terce,

Sext, None, Vespers, Compline, and Night Vigils (see Monday of the Fifth Week of Lent [Year C] and RB 8–19). Beside prayer, there is the time for work, simple meals, reading Scripture (*lectio divina*), and times of silence for private prayer and study.

BENEDICTINES IN EUROPE

Saint Benedict is known as the patriarch of western monasticism and co-patron of Europe because of the Benedictine role in missionizing pagan Europe. Augustine of Canterbury (who lived approximately two hundred years after Saint Augustine of Hippo, the great theologian), Saint Boniface, Saint Columbanus, and many others established monasteries and churches throughout Europe in the early medieval era. Benedictine monasteries, with their manuscript libraries, scriptoriums, and scholars, served as the primary educational centers of Europe in the Middle Ages. In fact, the Benedictine academy at the court of Charlemagne (742–814) was the rootstock of the great university system of later medieval Europe. Furthermore, Benedictines contributed to the economic and cultural advancement of Europe by their example of organized work, agriculture, focus on arts and sciences, and clear principles of government. The well-educated Benedictines were valued advisors to kings and princes.

The history of the Order of Saint Benedict in Europe begins in 595 when Pope Gregory sent Augustine of Canterbury to evangelize Britain. Augustine established a monastery at Canterbury, the first house for what would become a long and venerable tradition of Benedictine monasticism in the British Isles. In the seventh and eighth centuries, England sent Saints Willibrod and Boniface to be apostles to the Frisians (Netherlands) and Germans. Boniface established a multitude of churches and monasteries in what is now Germany; he became archbishop of Mainz, presided over councils, and anointed Pepin, Charlemagne's father, the King of the Franks. He is known as a Maker of Europe.

The seventh-century Irish monastic, Saint Columbanus, established monasteries throughout France and Italy while his disciple,

Gallus, established the monastery at Saint Gall's in Switzerland. The Abbey of Saint Gall was a chief center of learning in medieval Europe and the present-day Abbey has one of the most important collections of medieval manuscripts in the world. By the ninth century, the Rule of Benedict was the principal form of monasticism in Europe.

CLUNY

In 910, the Abbey of Cluny in Burgundy was established to reform the Benedictine order and for the next two centuries, Cluny was extremely influential in the western Church. By the twelfth century, Cluny was the head of the order with three hundred and fourteen monasteries located throughout Europe. The Cistercians (1098), Sylvestrines (1231), Celestines (1254), and others who also follow the Rule of Benedict are offshoots of the Cluny Benedictines.

SAINTS, SCHOLARS, APOSTLES, MARTYRS, AND POPES

The Order of Saint Benedict contributed martyrs, monks, missionaries, founders of abbeys, scholars, and popes (twenty-four) too numerous to mention to the life of the medieval Church but the short list must include Pope Gregory the Great of Rome; Saint Swithbert, the Apostle of Holland; Saint Dunstan, Abbot of Glastonbury; Saint Bede, historian and monk of Jarrow; Saint Anselm, monk, scholar and Archbishop of Canterbury; Alcuin of York, founder of the schools under Charlemagne; Saint Thomas of Canterbury (Thomas Becket), archbishop and martyr; Saint Hilda, Abbess of Whitby; Saint Hildegaard, musician, liturgist, and Abbess of Eisleben in Germany; and Peter the Venerable, ninth Abbot of Cluny.

LATE MEDIEVAL TO REFORMATION

With the rise of urbanization, the merchant classes, and the mendicant orders in the thirteenth century, the Order of Saint Benedict began a period of decline, although at the beginning of the fourteenth century there were as many as thirty-seven thousand Benedictine monasteries in Europe. Their decline quickened during the Reformation and the ensuing wars of religion in Europe when Benedictines experienced martyrdom, oppression, and exile. In England, Henry VIII dissolved the ancient monastic houses.

MODERN ERA

The order continued but did not really revive until the beginning of the present era when the modern age in need of spiritual guidance rediscovered the Benedictine practices of prayer and measured spiritual formation.

In 1883, Pope Leo XIII established the Benedictine Confederation, which oversees the order, and the College of Saint Anselm in Rome, which awards graduate degrees in theological studies for the education of Benedictines.

Today there are Benedictine houses throughout the world. In North America alone, there are over one hundred and fifty Benedictine communities that continue the venerable tradition of prayer, work, and hospitality in conjunction with apostolic endeavors in such fields as retreats and spiritual direction, evangelization, health care, and education. Europe has almost seven hundred Benedictine monasteries, while Asia, Africa, and Latin America each have more than one hundred.

All these monastic centers continue the important work of religious scholarship for which the Benedictines are known: they run high schools and elementary schools adjacent to their houses while their members teach at near-by universities and colleges or write or generally carry on the Benedictine tradition of education and research.

Benedictine monasteries serve as centers for a renewed life of prayer in the modern world. Since not everyone is called to a monastic life, the houses have oblates (from the Latin for "offer") attached to their monasteries. Oblates join in the life of prayer and service but do not take vows, choosing to remain in the world but following the Rule of Saint Benedict in their daily lives with the support of the monastic community. For example, one house in California has twenty-eight monks with five hundred oblates attached to it, which highlights the role the Order of Saint Benedict has in nourishing all those who seek God in the present era.

In conclusion, the Order of Saint Benedict continues the work of God in the world under the guidance of the ancient Rule. May the Rule of Saint Benedict guide your life of repentance and prayer in this Lenten season.

SUSAN E. BOND

Sources: George Cyprian Alston, "The Benedictine Order," in *The Catholic Encyclopedia*, vol. 2 (New York: Robert Appleton, 1907) available at New Advent http://newadvent.org/cathen (accessed August 8, 2009); Peter Brown, *The Rise of Western Christendom,* 2nd ed. (Malden, MA: Blackwell, 2003); Howard Clark Kee, et al., eds., *Christianity: A Social and Cutural History,* 2nd ed. (Upper Saddle River, NJ, 1998); the Web site of The Order of Saint Benedict available at www.osb.org (accessed August 8, 2009).

THE MEANING AND
CELEBRATION
OF LENT

For my friends and I when we were growing up, Lent was basically associated with three practices. First, we got out of school early on Fridays so that the Sisters could march all of us a mile to the church for the Stations of the Cross (this actually worked to my advantage because the church was only a block from my house). Second, we all gave up candy for Lent. Third, we raised and sent money to the missions. In our own young way, then, we were observing the three traditional Lenten practices of prayer, fasting, and almsgiving.

When I speak with people about Lent today, it sometimes seems that as a Church we have not gotten much beyond those three practices, if any of them are regularly practiced at all during the season of Lent. So as we prepare to use this book of daily meditations during this most holy season, it is good for us to reflect on Lent and what it means for us as individuals, as members of a parish, and as a Church which claims to be founded on and to rejoice in the teachings and redemptive work of Jesus Christ.

WHAT IS LENT?

Lent, a word of Germanic origin that simply means "spring," is used now to refer to that period of forty days that precede Easter. Those days are intended to be a time for us to prepare ourselves spiritually, mentally, and physically for the great celebration of the Paschal Feast that commemorates the death and rising to new life of our Lord and Savior Jesus Christ. References to a period of intense preparation for Easter can be found in some of the earliest writings of the Church. Later it was universally agreed that the time of Lent should be forty days based on the scriptural descriptions of the forty-day preparations of Moses (Exodus 34:28), Elijah (1 Kings 19:8), and Jesus (Matthew 4:1-2) before significant events in their lives. The Latin term for Lent, *Quadragesima*, in fact means forty days.

WHY DO WE OBSERVE LENT?

The first answer is the simple answer: we observe Lent, indeed, we need a time period like Lent, because we are sinners and the power of sin does not diminish. We regularly need to renew our conversion to the Lord by our turning away from sin. God calls us to walk in the way of his Son Jesus and we probably and sincerely want to do that, but the trials and temptations of daily life usually turn our attention away from the teachings of Jesus. We get caught up with dealing with all manner of problems and issues, and sometimes we just want to relax and get away from the push and pull of the demands of family, work, school, community, Church, and God. But God's call knows no time, it accepts no excuses, it brooks no shortcuts. Sin must be avoided in every instance. Lent reminds us of the awfulness of sin and the need to move away from it in response to the grace of God which invites us each day to take up our cross and follow in the footsteps of Jesus. This reason for a good Lenten observance is the main thrust of the readings at Mass for the first three weeks of Lent when Jesus reminds us of our sins and calls us to repentance and conversion.

A second answer to the question of why we need to observe Lent is found in the Mass readings for the final three weeks of Lent. In these readings, as we approach Holy Week and the Easter Triduum (that is, "three days") of Holy Thursday, Good Friday, and Holy Saturday leading up to Easter Sunday, we experience once again the great love and sacrifice that Jesus offered for our redemption. We follow him on his way to his destiny in Jerusalem; we watched the religious leaders of his day plot against him; we see the betrayal of Judas, the denial of Peter, and the desertion by the other apostles. In these readings we are given the opportunity to reflect once again on his agony in the Garden of Gethsemani, his arrest, trial and torture, his way of the cross to Golgatha, his death and burial. We need to renew our understanding and appreciation of what Jesus has done for us in a clear and, yes, even a dramatic way, for we are called upon to show that same kind of love to all people, especially to our enemies.

So there are two very good reasons for a careful and intense observance of Lent: as a reminder of our sinfulness and our need for conversion; as a reminder of the loving and freely offered sacrifice of Jesus for our redemption

HOW DO WE OBSERVE LENT?

Throughout the history of the Catholic Church, there have been many practices and exercises associated with Lent. Traditionally there are three ways that have persisted through the centuries. In his message for Lent in 2003, Pope John Paul II wrote: "Lent is a season of intense prayer, fasting, and concern for those in need. It offers all Christians an opportunity to prepare for Easter by serious discernment about their lives, with particular attention to the word of God which enlightens the daily journey of all who believe." Here the Holy Father sets out clearly the three basic elements of the Lenten observance: prayer, fasting, and almsgiving. These elements are grounded in the teachings of

Jesus in Matthew 6:1–6, 16–18 (see the Gospel for Ash Wednesday), the very first day of Lent. Let us take a moment to reflect on the general meaning of each one of these.

PRAYER

To pray is to address our thoughts, concerns, hopes, desires, and cares to God, to Jesus, to the Blessed Mother, or to a particular saint. To pray is to take some time during the day to offer praise for the goodness and love of God, to offer thanks for the many blessings and favors we have received, to ask for intercession for those persons or in those situations where there are serious difficulties (illness, marital troubles, etc.), or to ask pardon and forgiveness for our sins. Each Christian needs to find a form of prayer that is most helpful to her or him. And there are so many that have been used over these two millennia since the coming of Christ. Some use traditional prayers, like the Our Father and the Hail Mary; some say the rosary; some use devotional booklets of which they are fond; some like the official prayer of the Church, called the Liturgy of the Hours, which is based primarily on the Psalms from the Hebrew Scriptures; some prefer to be still and silent and simply repeat a simple sentence or word, such as the venerable Jesus Prayer ("Lord Jesus, son of the living God, have mercy on me, a sinner"). During Lent, the devotion of the Stations of the Cross can be very beneficial. For us Benedictines, and by extension for all Christians, Saint Benedict strongly urges the practice of spiritual reading (he called it *lectio divina*) or the prayerful meditation and reflection on the Bible and other spiritual works as the basis for prayer, as we shall explain the next section of the introduction.

A traditional sequence of prayer which has been passed down through the Christian ages and finds its roots in the monastic tradition, especially in the practice of spiritual reading, is very helpful for people as they develop their prayer life and one that you might want to consider. It is as follows: reading, meditation, prayer, and contemplation. Reading is not studying the text for the sake of knowledge, but listening to the Word of God as it speaks to us in the scriptures and other religious writings. After reading, one meditates on the message of the text to draw out its implications for our lives as Christians. In meditation we seek to let the text, the Word of God, enter more deeply into our consciousness and our everyday lives. Prayer is our response to the meditation, it is our turning to God to praise him, thank him, express sorrow for our sins, ask for his assistance as we strive to make the Word of God a more integral part of our lives.

Finally there is contemplation: this is a period of simply enjoying being in God's presence, just as one enjoys being in the presence of someone we love very deeply. There is no need for words; we simply want to be in God's presence.

The sequence takes a lot of practice and even the greatest of saints have attested to the difficulty of learning how to pray well. But each of us should feel an obligation to become better at prayer so that we might be better at being Christians. Lent is a wonderful time to discipline ourselves to practice prayer and to seek to grow in our love for prayer.

FASTING AND ABSTAINING

The second principal practice of Lent is fasting. This, too, is a practice that has always been associated with Lent. It is a way of disciplining the body and its many appetites for food, drink, and pleasures of any sort so that we can focus our minds and hearts on the love of God and the redemptive acts of Jesus. It is also a means of mortification, that is, of gaining control over our behavior, again so that we might devote ourselves more properly to hearing and doing the will of God. We fast when on a given day we take only one main meal, the other meal or meals of that day not being equal in amount to the main meal. The two main days of fasting in the Church are Ash Wednesday and Good Friday, but Christians are encouraged to fast on all the Fridays of Lent as well.

Another practice of Lent that sometimes gets confused with fasting is abstinence. Abstinence is giving up or not partaking in a specific kind of food. The most common form of abstinence is abstinence from meat. Thus the days of fasting mentioned above are also days of abstinence from meat (Ash Wednesday and Good Friday). Christians are further asked to abstain from meat on all the Fridays of Lent. We monks generally practice fasting and abstaining on a regular basis. In my community, for example, we abstain from meat on Wednesdays and Fridays throughout the year, except during the Christmas and Easter seasons, and we are encourage to abstain from other foods during Lent (see the reflection for Friday after Ash Wednesday for a humorous example of a Lenten abstinence).

However one wants to look at it, fasting and abstinence are essential aspects of Lent and we ought to find ways to use these venerable practices to help us prepare for Easter.

ALMSGIVING

Finally a word about almsgiving, which Pope Paul II described as "concern for those in need." This practice, like the other two, has roots in the Scriptures. It is one of the practices mentioned by Jesus in the Gospel for Ash Wednesday and thus has the weight of the Word of God behind it as something that Christians should do. Further, we know from the Acts of the Apostles that the early Christian community in Jerusalem was often in great distress because of the precarious situation it was in, but it strove to take care of all its members needs. Those on missionary journeys, like Saint Paul, would often ask their congregations to send donations and support to the Jerusalem community.

So we are asked during Lent to be especially mindful of those less fortunate than ourselves. There are many ways to fulfill this practice of Lent: volunteering in soup kitchens, helping with clothing and other drives, offering of time, talent, and treasure to Catholic Charities and other social agencies, and so on.

CELEBRATING LENT

This section of the introduction is entitled the Meaning and Celebration of Lent. I hope that the meaning is clear as a holy time of spiritual, mental, and physical preparation for Easter. I also hope that the notion of celebration has been conveyed as well. Lent is not meant to be an onerous burden, but as Saint Benedict would have it, a time during which we observe the practices of Lent all the while looking forward to holy Easter with joy and spiritual longing (see RB 49.7), and not only a particular Easter in a given year, but the eternal Easter where we hope to live in eternity with Christ Jesus and all the saints and all our loved ones.

The Stations of the Cross, giving up candy, money for the missions: these were the ways my friends and I practiced Lent in our youth. Perhaps that was not really a bad start. Hopefully as we mature, we can enter more deeply into the celebration of Lent as we grow in our relationship with the Lord in our life of prayer, as our fasting and abstaining become ways of freeing ourselves from unhelpful dependencies, and as our almsgiving opens us to the blessings of helping those in need in imitation of Christ.

REV. JOHN R. FORTIN, O.S.B.

SAINT BENEDICT
ON PRAYER
AND LENT

There are three principal forms of prayer for Saint Benedict. The first of these, to which he devotes several chapters in his Rule, is what he called the *Opus Dei*, the Work of God (not to be confused with the contemporary religious organization that has adopted this name). *Opus Dei* is also known as the Divine Office, the official prayer of the Church. For Saint Benedict, as for all authors of monastic rules, the communal recitation of the *Opus Dei* constituted a major part of the monastic day. The monks gathered for prayer eight times during the day, beginning with Vigils in the very early hours of the morning and concluding in the early evening with Night Prayer or Compline. The prayer services occurred at regular intervals during the day to sanctify the day and to remind the monks of the abiding and loving presence of God into whose service they had entered. These prayer hours consisted primarily of the recitation of the Psalms of the Old Testament, supplemented with canticles from the Old and New Testaments and readings from the Scriptures and respected Patristic authors.

The prayer that is central to Benedict's *Opus Dei* is the Lord's Prayer. In chapter 13 of his Rule, Benedict indicates that the Lord's Prayer is to be recited aloud by the superior at the end of Lauds and of Vespers, the two principal hours of praise which are celebrated in the morning and evening respectively. At the other hours of the day, the prayer is said in silence by all the monks and "only the last part of this prayer should be enunciated so that all may answer: 'But deliver us from evil.'" Benedict confirms this customary monastic practice in his Rule because forgiveness is so essential to the common life where the brothers are not exempt from what he calls "the thorns of contention" that are likely to arise among the brothers who live together so closely.

In the context of the public, communal life of prayer in the monastery, we probably should mention that Mass was celebrated only on Sundays and great feast days in Benedict's monastery, as daily Mass was not a practice until later in the history of the Church. Benedict himself was not a priest and his monastic rule was intended primarily for laymen. There were a few priests in the community to take care of the sacramental needs of the monks, but otherwise they were expected to follow the Rule just like everyone else.

The second principal form of prayer for Saint Benedict was *lectio divina* or spiritual reading, the slow and careful reading of and meditation on the Scriptures discussed above. In the daily schedule, which he presents in chapter 48 of his Rule, it is clear that Benedict expects the monks to spend several hours each day doing *lectio divina* in addition to the time spent in choir reciting the *Opus Dei*. The work that needs to be done in the monastery and the times for meals are scheduled around the times for the *Opus Dei* and *lectio divina*. On Sundays, the monks are to spend most of the day, apart from the *Opus Dei* and common meals, doing *lectio divina*.

The third principal form of prayer in Benedict's monastery is private prayer. This prayer takes place whenever the monk is moved by the Spirit of God. It can take place while at work, while listening to the reading during meals, even while in choir, and perhaps especially when doing *lectio divina*. Benedict mentions, for example, in chapter 52 on the church or oratory of the monastery that when the time for the *Opus Dei* is over the monks are to leave quietly so that someone "who may wish to pray by himself not be hindered." He also says that nothing else is to be kept or done in the oratory except the *Opus Dei* so that "if someone perhaps wishes to pray privately at some other time, [he may] simply go in and pray." Benedict gives no specific instructions or teachings about private prayer, leaving it to each monk to develop his own form of intimate communication with the Lord, but Benedict clearly believed in the necessity of the *Opus Dei* and of *lectio divina* for private prayer to be fruitful and based on a sound faith.

Saint Benedict does not talk about meditation or contemplation in his Rule. It is quite possible that the teachings of Patristic writers from the early centuries of the Church, such as Cassian and Origen and Saint Basil, provided the material for such teaching. Nonetheless, it is clear that the life of the monk in his monastery, with its daily practices of the *Opus Dei*, *lectio divina*, and private prayer, led the monks into deeper and deeper relationships with the Lord and perhaps even wordless communion with Him in the powerful presence of His divine love. Certainly, Benedict himself experienced this during his lifetime, as his biographer Saint Gregory attests in chapter 35 of his life of Saint Benedict (see Suggestions for Further Reading).

The Gospel for Ash Wednesday, from Saint Matthew's account of the Sermon on the Mount, sets out for us the three traditional practices for those who seek to repent for sins of the past and to prepare themselves well for the celebration of Easter. Those practices are prayer, fasting, and almsgiving (Mt 6:1–6, 16–18). During Lent, it is customary for Catholics to pray more often by attending daily Mass, participating in weekly Stations of the Cross and Lenten penance services, attending parish missions, and so on.

In the tradition of the Church, prayer has always had a central place in the season of Lent. For Saint Benedict, prayer is not only a central feature of the monastic life but also an especially important part of Lenten practice. In chapter 49 of the Rule, "The Observance of Lent,"

Benedict speaks of the need to "devote ourselves to tearful prayer" (that is, prayer seeking forgiveness for sins committed in the past) and of the importance of "increasing the regular measure of our service [the Divine Office] in the form of special prayers" during Lent.

For Benedict, the purpose of Lent is not to provide an opportunity for the monks to try to become spiritual and ascetic athletes, capable of severe fasts, long hours of prayer, and so forth. Rather he invites the monks, with the express permission of the abbot, to take on penitential exercises. Since ultimately the purpose of Lent is to help the monk learn to "await Holy Easter with the joy of spiritual desire," so, too, is the practice of Lenten prayer ordered to the goal of experiencing the glorious wonder of the Lord's Resurrection at Easter and throughout the year.

This book offers a unique way to pray during Lent by offering the reader the Gospel for each day of Lent, followed by a quote from the Rule of Saint Benedict and a brief reflection, concluding with a prayer appropriate to the day. The advantage of this format is that it invites the reader to pray over the revealed Word of God under the guidance of a truly great spiritual Master. Saint Benedict did not write his own reflections of the Scriptures, but at least one third of the Rule consists of direct or indirect citations of the Scriptures, showing that Benedict was indeed a man who thought and spoke and breathed the words of Jesus, and desired others to come to know the joy and peace of prayer.

You are therefore invited by Jesus and Saint Benedict to read prayerfully and slowly each day of the Lent and Holy Week the Gospel passage, the quote from Saint Benedict's Rule, and the reflection. As you consider the messages, you are invited to conclude your meditation with a prayer, either with the prayers offered here or one in your own words as the Spirit inspires you.

And as you journey through Lent, may you come to Holy Easter "with the joy of spiritual desire."

REV. JOHN R. FORTIN, O.S.B.

ON THE DAILY
GOSPEL READINGS

As noted, this book presents daily readings and prayers for every day of Lent, weekdays, and Sundays. The daily readings begin with a Gospel Reading, followed by a quote from Saint Benedict's Rule, a reflection, and a prayer.

The Gospel Readings are from the Roman Catholic *Lectionary for Mass for Use in the Dioceses of the United States of America*. The Lectionary for Mass contains the readings for Mass selected from the Bible.

If you were to attend daily Mass during Lent in the United States, you would hear the same Daily Gospel Readings included in this book. For example, the Ash Wednesday Gospel Reading, Matthew 6:1–6, 16–18, is the same Gospel Reading you would hear when you attend Mass to receive your ashes. In fact, on each day at all the Masses of the Latin-rite Roman Catholic Church throughout the world, the same readings are heard in Mass, read in the vernacular language or Latin.

There are two main components of the Lectionary: Sunday and Weekday readings. Sunday readings are arranged on a three-year cycle:

Year A, Year B, and Year C. The Gospel Readings for Year A are generally from the Gospel of St. Matthew, Year B are generally from the Gospel of St. Mark and Year C are generally from Gospel of St. Luke. St. John's Gospel is read on Sundays in Year A, B, and C during specific liturgical calendar periods.

The Weekday readings are on a two-year cycle: Year I and Year II. Year I are odd-numbered years and Year II are even-numbered years. However, the Weekday readings during Lent are the same for Year I and Year II but differ each day. In the book, the Weekday Gospel Readings are also the Weekday Gospel Readings in the Lectionary.

For Sundays in this book, you have three different selections of readings and prayers. Each selection begins with a different Gospel Reading, the Gospel Reading from Year A, B, or C of the Lectionary.

Appendix A, the Calendar for Lent 2010–2019 & Lectionary Cycle, lists the specific dates for the next ten years for Ash Wednesday, the Sundays of Lent, and includes the Sunday Lectionary Cycle for the year. Please refer to the table to determine the current year's Sunday Lectionary Cycle: Year A, B, or C and select the appropriate Sunday reading for the present year.

This book in a small way invites you to pray each day with the Church and your fellow Christians in the world on your Lenten Journey with Jesus Christ and Saint Benedict.

PETER J. MONGEAU

"We should also realize that it is not in much talking that we shall be heard, but in purity of heart and tearful compunction. Therefore prayer should be short and pure, unless perhaps it be prolonged under the inspiration of divine grace."

(RB) 20.3–4

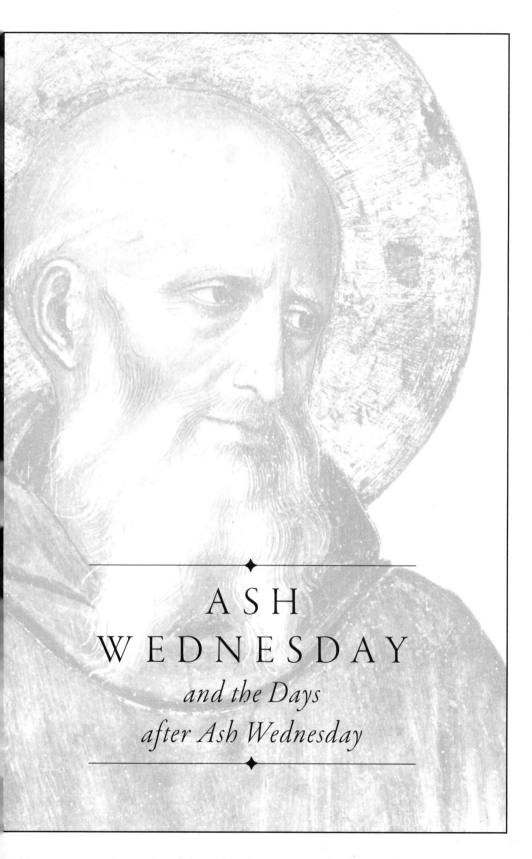

ASH WEDNESDAY

*and the Days
after Ash Wednesday*

GOSPEL

JESUS SAID TO HIS DISCIPLES:

"Take care not to perform righteous deeds in order that people may see them; otherwise, you will have no recompense from your heavenly Father. When you give alms, do not blow a trumpet before you, as the hypocrites do in the synagogues and in the streets to win the praise of others. Amen, I say to you, they have received their reward. But when you give alms, do not let your left hand know what your right is doing, so that your almsgiving may be secret. And your Father who sees in secret will repay you.

"When you pray, do not be like the hypocrites, who love to stand and pray in the synagogues and on street corners so that others may see them. Amen, I say to you, they have received their reward. But when you pray, go to your inner room, close the door, and pray to your Father in secret. And your Father who sees in secret will repay you.

"When you fast, do not look gloomy like the hypocrites. They neglect their appearance, so that they may appear to others to be fasting. Amen, I say to you, they have received their reward. But when you fast, anoint your head and wash your face, so that you may not appear to be fasting, except to your Father who is hidden. And your Father who sees what is hidden will repay you."

MATTHEW 6: 1-6, 16-18

SAINT BENEDICT

"We urge them to guard their lives with all purity during these Lenten days. All should work together at effacing during this holy season the negligences of other times."

RB 49.2–3

REFLECTION

Saint Benedict sets forth for his monks and for all of us the two-fold task of any genuine Lenten observance: to strive to purify one's life and to wash away the guilt of sin. This task is indeed one task, for in purifying one's life, in cooperating with the grace of God to grow in holiness by seeking to love God and neighbor more and more, one is indeed learning how one's sins may be washed away: that is, by giving oneself over to the healing and saving love of Jesus Christ. This begins with an inner conversion that manifests itself in outer actions that reflect the teaching of Jesus in today's Gospel.

We are to give alms, to pray, and to fast not with a view to recognition by others or to self-adulation for a job well done ("I did pretty well passing up dessert at dinner today"), but with a view to doing these deeds as purely as possible, that is, from the single motive of a sincere desire to love God with all our heart, soul, strength, and will.

PRAYER

Lord God of heaven and earth, today in a special way you call us to remember who we are, formed out of dust and ashes yet quickened and enlivened by the breath of your very Spirit, so that we might become who we are destined by you to be: citizens of heaven and co-heirs with Christ. Grant us the grace to enter into the mystery of this holy season of Lent with hearts yearning to be cleansed of sin so that purified in thought, word, and deed we may truly and deeply love you and all others in you. We ask this through the merits of your Son, Jesus Christ, who suffered and died for us. Amen.

GOSPEL

JESUS SAID TO HIS DISCIPLES:

"The Son of Man must suffer greatly and be rejected by the elders, the chief priests, and the scribes, and be killed and on the third day be raised."

Then he said to all, "If anyone wishes to come after me, he must deny himself and take up his cross daily and follow me. For whoever wishes to save his life will lose it, but whoever loses his life for my sake will save it. What profit is there for one to gain the whole world yet lose or forfeit himself?"

LUKE 9: 22-25

SAINT BENEDICT

"Thus you will return by the labor of obedience to the one from whom you drifted through the inertia of disobedience. Now then I address my words to you: whoever is willing to renounce self-will, and take up the powerful and shining weapons of obedience to fight for the Lord Christ, the true king."

RB PROLOGUE 2–3

REFLECTION

One of my uncles was fond of saying, "Growing old is not for the faint of heart." Neither is Lent and neither is the stark, powerful summons that Jesus issues in today's Gospel with its call to deny oneself and lose one's life. To take up one's cross daily and to follow Christ is to imitate Christ in his obedience to the will of the Father. We have drifted from God by our obedience to our own wills, whims, and desires; we gradually moved away from hearing his Word and have become attuned only to what is easy, what is pleasing, what is seemingly fulfilling.

We can return to the Lord, Jesus and Benedict teach us, but the way is narrow: it is traversed only by struggle, by effort, by battle fought with the weapons of obedience to the Word graciously given us by the Lord. We can return to the Lord only by conforming our lives to the person of Jesus Christ.

PRAYER

Heavenly Father, you have destined us to be among your saints in heaven, but you ask us to cooperate with the grace you have given us in Christ Jesus and to take up our cross each day, fearful of its burden and weight but confident that in Christ it is a burden that by his favor and love is light and easy. We make this pray through Christ our Lord. Amen.

GOSPEL

The disciples of John approached Jesus and said, "Why do we and the Pharisees fast much, but your disciples do not fast?" Jesus answered them, "Can the wedding guests mourn as long as the bridegroom is with them? The days will come when the bridegroom is taken away from them, and then they will fast."

MATTHEW 9: 14-15

SAINT BENEDICT

"Finally, during Lent and until Easter, they should eat in the evening."
RB 41.7

REFLECTION

One of the monks here at the abbey drew a hearty chuckle from the congregation one Sunday in Lent when he began his homily by announcing that he was giving up watermelon for Lent. His wry remark led into a soul-searching and quite serious reflection on the whole meaning of fasting. For Saint Benedict, a fast day meant that the monks had their main meal in the evening, being sustained through the day only by a small noon repast.

We need to be reminded of the two lessons about fasting. The first lesson is that through fasting we begin to live in greater solidarity with the Lord who suffered and died for us, who gave up all, including his place at the right hand of the Father, for us (Phil 2:6–11). The second lesson is that through fasting we can begin to be empowered to love God and his people with renewed energy and clarity. All this thanks to the grace of God.

PRAYER

Heavenly Father, help us in this Lent to practice the penance of fasting with joyful hearts, for you love a cheerful giver. May we thus be prepared in body and soul to celebrate the Passover Supper of the Eucharist and be strengthened in our faith in the Resurrection of your beloved Son, who lives and reigns with you and the Holy Spirit, one God forever and ever. Amen.

GOSPEL

Jesus saw a tax collector named Levi sitting at the customs post. He said to him, "Follow me." And leaving everything behind, he got up and followed him. Then Levi gave a great banquet for him in his house, and a large crowd of tax collectors and others were at table with them. The Pharisees and their scribes complained to his disciples, saying, "Why do you eat and drink with tax collectors and sinners?" Jesus said to them in reply, "Those who are healthy do not need a physician, but the sick do. I have not come to call the righteous to repentance but sinners."

LUKE 5: 27-32

SAINT BENEDICT

"Listen, O my son, to the teachings of your master, and turn to them with the ear of your heart. Willingly accept the advice of a devoted father and put it into practice."

RB PROLOGUE 1

REFLECTION

When Jesus called to Levi the tax collector, Levi heard his name as he had never heard it before. So often in the past others had called to him: "Levi, let's go party." "Levi, when are you inviting us over for a drink?" "Levi, you're so clever. How do you get away with it?" But the voice that called to him on that day was a voice which penetrated his shallow exterior and, like a two-edged sword separating bone from marrow, entered into his heart of hearts and summoned him to realize, acknowledge, and confront the truth about himself: that he was a sinner in need of divine healing and forgiveness.

Saint Benedict issues a similar call and reminds us that in this holy season of Lent we have an opportunity to hear the Lord call our names again as if for the first time and to respond obediently, humbly and generously: "If today you hear his voice, harden not your hearts" (Ps 95:7).

PRAYER

Almighty God, from the dawn of creation and even now you call to your children, made in your image and likeness, to answer your summons to walk with you, our loving Father, in the garden. Grant us the grace to listen for your voice each day of our lives and to respond with love in imitation of Christ: "Speak, for your servant is listening" (1 Sm 3:10). We make this prayer through the same Christ our Lord. Amen.

FIRST WEEK
OF
LENT

GOSPEL

At that time Jesus was led by the Spirit into the desert to be tempted by the devil. He fasted for forty days and forty nights, and afterwards he was hungry. The tempter approached and said to him, "If you are the Son of God, command that these stones become loaves of bread."

He said in reply, "It is written: / *One does not live on bread alone, / but on every word that comes forth from the mouth of God.*" / Then the devil took him to the holy city, and made him stand on the parapet of the temple, and said to him, "If you are the Son of God, throw yourself down. For it is written: / *He will command his angels concerning you / and with their hands they will support you, / lest you dash your foot against a stone.*" / Jesus answered him, "Again it is written, *You shall not put the Lord, your God, to the test.*" Then the devil took him up to a very high mountain, and showed him all the kingdoms of the world in their magnificence, and he said to him, "All these I shall give to you, if you will prostrate yourself and worship me." At this, Jesus said to him, "Get away, Satan! It is written: / *The Lord, your God, shall you worship / and him alone shall you serve.*" / Then the devil left him and, behold, angels came and ministered to him.

MATTHEW 4: 1-11

SAINT BENEDICT

"When the wicked one, the devil, suggests something, [the monk] pushes both him and his advice out of the sight of his heart; he annihilates the satanic incipient thoughts, taking them and smashing them against Christ."

RB PROLOGUE 28

REFLECTION

The call to the desert is strong in the monastic tradition and indeed it was that call that inspired the early Christian monks to leave everything behind and go to the deserted places to confront the devils in themselves. There they learned that the hard and rugged path to God's holy mountain could be followed, narrow though it may be, when they put their whole trust in God and when they made Christ truly the center and source of meaning of their lives.

Lent is an invitation to assume that same attitude, an invitation to the barrenness of the desert where one can find the beauty of God's grace, where one can encounter the Lord who makes our crosses and trials and temptations light and easy only if we shoulder his yoke, his burden, and his cross as well, and dash all that comes from the tempter against him who is our Rock and our Savior.

PRAYER

Heavenly Father, you patiently call us to respond to your grace and offer us the promise of your Son that he will indeed be with us always until the end of time. Grant us the grace to confront the evils within ourselves, to seek forgiveness, and to walk with all our sisters and brothers in newness of life. Grant this through Christ our Lord. Amen.

GOSPEL

The Spirit drove Jesus out into the desert, and he remained in the desert for forty days, tempted by Satan. He was among wild beasts, and the angels ministered to him.

After John had been arrested, Jesus came to Galilee proclaiming the gospel of God: "This the time of fulfillment. The kingdom of God is at hand. Repent, and believe in the gospel."

MARK 1: 12-15

SAINT BENEDICT

"The basic road to progress for the humble person is through prompt obedience. This is characteristic of those who hold Christ more precious than all else."

RB 5.1–2

REFLECTION

There is simply no getting around the truth, that stark and sometimes very intimidating truth, that all humans are subject to temptation and that there are no respites from this reality. It is a battle and it is life-long. Christ himself, enduring for forty days a strict regimen of fasting and prayer in the desert, where he had been led by the Spirit, was not exempt from this universal evil challenger to those who are blessed with free will. Christ overcame the three temptations for one simple reason: he came to do the Father's will and he never betrayed or abandoned that commitment.

Saint Benedict understands this and so his call to prompt and ready obedience to the will of the Father uses a military metaphor to highlight the struggle there will be even for those who take up "the powerful and shining weapons of obedience to fight for the Lord." Christians enter the desert of temptation with grace-filled confidence because of their hope in the promise of Christ: "My mother and my brothers are those who hear the word of God and act on it" (Lk 8:21).

PRAYER

Our Father in heaven, we believe that Christ became human like us in all things but sin. Hear our prayers and be merciful to us, that in time of temptation and trial we may know your presence and your peace. We make this prayer through Christ our Lord. Amen.

GOSPEL

Filled with the Holy Spirit, Jesus returned from the Jordan and was led by the Spirit into the desert for forty days, to be tempted by the devil. He ate nothing during those days, and when they were over he was hungry. The devil said to him, "If you are the Son of God, command this stone to become bread." Jesus answered him, "It is written, *One does not live on bread alone.*" Then he took him up and showed him all the kingdoms of the world in a single instant. The devil said to him, "I shall give to you all this power and glory; for it has been handed over to me, and I may give it to whomever I wish. All this will be yours, if you worship me." Jesus said to him in reply, "It is written: / *You shall worship the Lord, your God, and him alone shall you serve.*" / Then he led them to Jerusalem, made him stand on the parapet of the temple, and said to him, "If you are the Son of God, throw yourself down from here, for it is written: / *He will command his angels concerning you, to guard you,* / and: / *With their hands they will support you,* / *lest you dash your foot against a stone.*" / Jesus said to him in reply, "It also says, *You shall not put the Lord, your God, to the test.*" When the devil had finished every temptation, he departed from him for a time.

LUKE 4: 1-13

SAINT BENEDICT

"That is why they do not wish to live by their own lights, obeying their own desires and wants. Rather, they prefer to walk according to the judgment and command of another . . . Doubtless, people such as these imitate the Lord who said: 'I did not come to do my own will, but the will of the one who sent me.'"

RB 5.12AB, 13

REFLECTION

When Christ confronted evil and threats in the lives of others, his reactions were swift and sure. At his word evil demons fled in confusion and outrage, all manner of illnesses and diseases were healed and the sick restored to health, storms and tempests at sea were calmed, thousands were fed on a few loaves and fish, and even death was turned back on itself. But in the desert, alone and fasting forty days, when Christ confronted evil aimed at himself, he did nothing. Yes, he responded with the words of Scripture to the temptations of the devil, but he did not act. It was as if he knew and loved the will of God so much that he would not invoke divine power unless the will of God commanded it.

Saint Benedict teaches us that our call to discipleship asks no less of us. With God's grace, we are to confront evil relying solely on God's power and promise that nothing can separate us from his love made visible in Christ Jesus our Lord (Rm 8:35–39).

PRAYER

Lord Jesus Christ, you offered your whole being to the Father for our salvation. May we in this season of Lent learn what it means to serve you with our whole heart, soul, strength, and will. You live and reign with the Father and the Holy Spirit forever and ever. Amen.

GOSPEL

Jesus said to his disciples:

"When the Son of Man comes in his glory, and all the angels with him, he will sit upon his glorious throne, and all the nations will be assembled before him. And he will separate them one from another, as a shepherd separates the sheep from the goats. He will place the sheep on his right and the goats on his left. Then the king will say to those on his right, 'Come, you who are blessed by my Father. Inherit the kingdom prepared for you from the foundation of the world. For I was hungry and you gave me food, I was thirsty and you gave me drink, a stranger and you welcomed me, naked and you clothed me, ill and you cared for me, in prison and you visited me.' Then the righteous will answer him and say, 'Lord, when did we see you hungry and feed you, or thirsty and give you drink? When did we see you a stranger and welcome you, or naked and clothe you? When did we see you ill or in prison, and visit you?' And the king will say to them in reply, 'Amen, I say to you, whatever you did for one of these least brothers of mine, you did for me.' Then he will say to those on his left, 'Depart from me, you accursed, into the eternal fire prepared for the Devil and his angels. For I was hungry and you gave me no food, I was thirsty and you gave me no drink, a stranger and you gave me no welcome, naked and you gave me no clothing, ill and in prison, and you did not care for me.' Then they will answer and say, 'Lord, when did we see you hungry or thirsty or a stranger or naked or ill or in prison, and not minister to your needs?' He will answer them, 'Amen, I say to you, what you did not do for one of these least ones, you did not do for me.' And these will go off to eternal punishment, but the righteous to eternal life."

Matthew 25: 31-46

SAINT BENEDICT

"The sick are to be cared for before and above all else, for it is really Christ who is served in them. He himself said: I was sick and you visited me, *and* Whatever you did to one of these little ones, you did to me." *"All guests who arrive should be received as Christ, for he himself will say,* I was a stranger and you took me in."

RB 36.1–3; RB 53.1

REFLECTION

The words of the final judgment scene in Saint Matthew's Gospel often evoke images of weeping and wailing and grinding of teeth, the result of not doing the simple acts of charity that Christ enumerates: feeding the hungry, giving drink to the thirsty, and so on. But when Saint Benedict reads this Gospel he finds in it opportunities: here is how I can serve the Lord and I so want to serve the Lord. Thus he cites this Gospel passage in places where one might not expect to find it: in the chapter on caring for the sick and in the chapter on serving guests. These simple deeds performed for Christ and performed in Christ are for the building up of the kingdom of God.

Lent affords us an opportunity to redirect our efforts and talent so that we might more closely conform our attitudes and deeds to those of Christ.

PRAYER

Hear our prayer, O Lord, and have mercy on us. Gladden our hearts with your grace that we may joyfully serve you by serving the needs of all our sisters and brothers, for in helping to bind their wounds we touch your wounded hands, feet, and side, and so are blessed beyond measure. You live and reign with the Father and the Holy Spirit forever and ever. Amen.

GOSPEL

JESUS SAID TO HIS DISCIPLES:

"In praying, do not babble like the pagans, who think that they will be heard because of their many words. Do not be like them. Your Father knows what you need before you ask him.

"This is how you are to pray:

Our Father who art in heaven,
hallowed be thy name,
thy Kingdom come,
thy will be done,
on earth as it is in heaven.
Give us this day our daily bread;
and forgive us our trespasses,
as we forgive those who trespass against us;
and lead us not into temptation,
but deliver us from evil.

"If you forgive men their transgressions, your heavenly Father will forgive you. But if you do not forgive men, neither will your Father forgive your transgressions."

MATTHEW 6: 7-15

SAINT BENEDICT

"The celebration of Matins and Vespers must certainly never transpire without the superior concluding with the complete Lord's Prayer while all the rest listen. This is done because of the thorns of quarreling that often spring up."

RB 13.12–13

REFLECTION

Saint Benedict directs that, at the conclusion of the major hours of the Divine Office, the superior is to recite the Lord's Prayer aloud as the monks bow in silence and unite their hearts and minds to the words prayed over them by that single voice who speaks for all in saying the words of the Our Father. Forgiveness lies at the heart of the Christian faith and is, perhaps, one of the greatest gifts Christians can offer the world, which is so often bent on revenge and vengeance.

"Thorns of quarreling" can arise anywhere and anytime, at home or at work, at school or at play, but so, too, can the Lord's Prayer arise from our lips and in our hearts to remind us of the Lord's admonition and invitation: forgive that you may be forgiven. Thus may we be cleansed of ours sins; thus may we be disciples who offer the Lord's gift of cleansing and forgiveness.

PRAYER

Our Father, who art in heaven, hallowed by thy name. Thy kingdom come, thy will be done on earth as it is in heaven. Give us this day our daily bread, and forgive us our trespasses as we forgive those who trespass against us. And lead us not into temptation but deliver us from evil. Amen.

GOSPEL

While still more people gathered in the crowd, Jesus said to them, "This generation is an evil generation; it seeks a sign, but no sign will be given it, except the sign of Jonah. Just as Jonah became a sign to the Ninevites, so will the Son of Man be to this generation. At the judgment the queen of the south will rise with the men of this generation and she will condemn them, because she came from the ends of the earth to hear the wisdom of Solomon, and there is something greater than Solomon here. At the judgment the men of Nineveh will arise with this generation and condemn it, because at the preaching of Jonah they repented, and there is something greater than Jonah here."

LUKE 11: 29-32

SAINT BENEDICT

"[The abbot] is believed to represent Christ in the monastery, for he is called by his name in accord with the saying of the Apostle: 'You have received the Spirit of adoption of children, in which we cry Abba, Father!'" (Rm 8:15).

RB 2.2–3

REFLECTION

A living sign of God's presence in a monastic community is the abbot or superior. According to Saint Benedict, the abbot is called upon to give witness to the Lord and his salvific mission by his teaching and by his example, thereby calling, leading, and encouraging the monks to make good on their vows of conversion, obedience, and stability (i.e., to live in the monastery of their profession for life). In all this the abbot draws on the model of Christ, whose call to repentance and whose ability to see into the hearts of his hearers drew so many to come to him and to follow him, as we read in the opening verse of today's Gospel: ". . . still more people gathered in the crowd."

The discipline of Lent is a time for repentance and conversion, a time to find in Christ that model and exemplar of the Christian life to which we have all vowed ourselves by our baptismal promises.

PRAYER

Lord Jesus, turn our hearts to you and grant us the gift of your divine Spirit that in all we say and do we may give witness and become signs to others of your love, forgiveness, and saving power. You are our Lord forever and ever. Amen.

GOSPEL

JESUS SAID TO HIS DISCIPLES:

"Ask and it will be given to you; seek and you will find; knock and the door will be opened to you. For everyone who asks, receives; and the one who seeks, finds; and to the one who knocks, the door will be opened. Which one of you would hand his son a stone when he asked for a loaf of bread, or a snake when he asked for a fish? If you then, who are wicked, know how to give good gifts to your children, how much more will your heavenly Father give good things to those who ask him.

"Do to others whatever you would have them do to you. This is the law and the prophets."

MATTHEW 7: 7-12

SAINT BENEDICT

"When we wish to propose something to powerful people, we do not presume to do so without humility and reverence. How much more should we petition the Lord God of the universe with great humility and total devotion. We should also realize that it is not in much talking that we shall be heard, but in purity of heart and tearful compunction."

RB 20.1–3

REFLECTION

Pure devotion, purity of heart, prayer that is short and pure: in three successive verses in chapter 20 of his Rule, Saint Benedict unequivocally unites purity and prayer. His intention perhaps is to remind us that ultimately the purpose of prayer is to clear our vision of all that is extraneous to being true, faithful disciples of Christ. What we genuinely need, what we ought to ask for, seek after, and knock on the door to obtain, is the courage to live in faith, hope, and love.

During this time of Lent, we pray in a special way that we might, with God's grace, strive to live as true disciples of Jesus Christ and fulfill our commitment to bringing his message of peace, forgiveness, and healing to the world by lives of humble, joyful, and, yes, pure service. The promise of the Beatitudes should enliven our resolve: "Blessed are the pure of heart, for they shall see God" (Mt 5:8).

PRAYER

Lord God of heaven and earth, you invite us into intimate union with you in prayer. May your image and likeness be perfected in us so that we may serve as your faithful and living witnesses in our day. We make this prayer through Christ our Lord. Amen.

GOSPEL

JESUS SAID TO HIS DISCIPLES:

"I tell you, unless your righteousness surpasses that of the scribes and Pharisees, you will not enter into the Kingdom of heaven.

"You have heard that it was said to your ancestors, *You shall not kill; and whoever kills will be liable to judgment.* But I say to you, whoever is angry with his brother will be liable to judgment, and whoever says to his brother, *Raqa,* will be answerable to the Sanhedrin, and whoever says, 'You fool,' will be liable to fiery Gehenna. Therefore, if you bring your gift to the altar, and there recall that your brother has anything against you, leave your gift there at the altar, go first and be reconciled with your brother, and then come and offer your gift. Settle with your opponent quickly while on the way to court. Otherwise your opponent will hand you over to the judge, and the judge will hand you over to the guard, and you will be thrown into prison. Amen, I say to you, you will not be released until you have paid the last penny."

MATTHEW 5: 20-26

SAINT BENEDICT

"Not to kill."

RB 4.3

REFLECTION

It might seem very strange that in his chapter on the tools for good works in his Rule for monks Saint Benedict would include the fifth commandment of the Decalogue, which Christ raises in today's Gospel: do not kill. Perhaps it was the case that Saint Benedict wanted to recall for his monks this and all the commandments of the Mosaic Law to remind them of all the history of the Chosen People and the new people formed by the New Covenant. Perhaps he wanted to encourage them to confront the hostility and anger that sometimes can reside in a person, even a vowed monk, and to admonish them to turn to the Lord and his grace for help, to move beyond "not to kill" to the more difficult and demanding new commandments Christ laid down for his disciples: "Love your enemies" (RB 4.31) and "Pray for your enemies for the love of Christ" (RB 4.72).

Perhaps he wanted to impress upon his monks the extent of love expected of them for God and neighbor, to call them to surpass the mere external observance of the law of the Lord and to enter more and more deeply into its true and essential meaning: the revelation of the life and love of the Blessed Trinity.

PRAYER

Lord God, without your grace we could never fulfill your commandments, especially your commandment to love, though we know it is the way of your Son. Grant us this grace, we humbly ask you, and lead us always to act in love as Christ has taught us. We make this prayer through the same Christ our Lord. Amen.

GOSPEL

JESUS SAID TO HIS DISCIPLES:

"You have heard that it was said, *You shall love your neighbor and hate your enemy.* But I say to you, love your enemies, and pray for those who persecute you, that you may be children of your heavenly Father, for he makes his sun rise on the bad and the good, and causes rain to fall on the just and the unjust. For if you love those who love you, what recompense will you have? Do not the tax collectors do the same? And if you greet your brothers and sisters only, what is unusual about that? Do not the pagans do the same? So be perfect, just as your heavenly Father is perfect."

MATTHEW 5: 43-48

SAINT BENEDICT

"Therefore, when he has climbed all these steps of humility, the monk will soon arrive at that perfect love of God which drives out fear."

RB 7.67

REFLECTION

Every Christian has the obligation to strive for the perfection to which Christ calls each of us. This striving is not reserved to a chosen few. Saint Paul described how this perfection could be achieved with God's grace in his letter to the Colossians: "Put on then, as God's chosen ones, holy and beloved, heartfelt compassion, kindness, humility, gentleness, and patience, bearing with one another and forgiving one another, if one has a grievance against another; as the Lord has forgiven you, so must you also do. And over all these put on love, that is, the bond of perfection" (Col 3:12–14).

As the Lord God "makes the sun to rise on the bad and the good, and causes rain to fall on the just and the unjust," so the love of each Christian is to rise for all and descend on all. The perfect love of God, the goal of all monastic practices according to Saint Benedict, is as well the perfect love of all God's people without qualification.

PRAYER

Heavenly Father, you so loved the world that you sent your only Son and you gave us this season of Lent so that we might expand our hearts in love and so become more and more like him. By your grace, may we continually grow in love. We ask this through Christ our Lord. Amen.

SECOND WEEK
OF
LENT

GOSPEL

Jesus took Peter, James, and John his brother, and led them up a high mountain by themselves. And he was transfigured before them; his face shone like the sun and his clothes became white as light. And behold, Moses and Elijah appeared to them, conversing with him. Then Peter said to Jesus in reply, "Lord, it is good that we are here. If you wish, I will make three tents here, one for you, one for Moses, and one for Elijah." While he was still speaking, behold, a bright cloud cast a shadow over them, then from the cloud came a voice that said, "This is my beloved Son, with whom I am well pleased; listen to him." When the disciples heard this, they fell prostrate and were very much afraid. But Jesus came and touched them, saying, "Rise, and do not be afraid." And when the disciples raised their eyes, they saw no one else but Jesus alone.

As they were coming down from the mountain, Jesus charged them, "Do not tell the vision to anyone until the Son of Man has been raised from the dead."

MATTHEW 17: 1-9

SAINT BENEDICT

"A senior should be assigned to [the novices] who is gifted in spiritual guidance and will observe them very carefully. One must note whether [the novice] really seeks God, and whether he is serious about the Word of God, obedience and hardships. He should be told all the hard and harsh things that lead to God."

RB 58.6–8

REFLECTION

Saint Benedict did not expect those who sought entrance into the monastery to be fully and completely formed as religious or as Christians. From his own experience in seeking God he knew that only over time and with a sincere heart and by the grace of God, guided by those knowledgeable in the ways of the Lord and supported by the monastic community, could an aspirant eventually come to be truly a "vir Dei," a man of God. All of us need this ongoing formation experience that we might be transformed more and more into the pattern of the Son of God.

Each year Lent affords us an opportunity to enter more deeply into that formative process. The Transfiguration reminds us of the glory that lies beyond the cross, yet that cross, our cross, what Saint Benedict would call "the hard and harsh things that lead to God," is not simply a hurdle to be overcome but a crucial characteristic of our living in the Spirit of Christ.

PRAYER

Free us, O Lord, from the darkness of pride and sin that surrounds us that we might enter into the radiant light of your love and goodness and mercy, and so become partakers of your divine kingdom. You live and reign forever and ever. Amen.

GOSPEL

Jesus took Peter, James and John and led them up a high mountain apart by themselves. And he was transfigured before them, and his clothes became dazzling white, such as no fuller on earth could bleach them. Then Elijah appeared to them along with Moses, and they were conversing with Jesus. Then Peter said to Jesus in reply, "Rabbi, it is good that we are here! Let us make three tents: one for you, one for Moses, and one for Elijah." He hardly knew what to say, they were so terrified. Then a cloud came, casting a shadow over them; from the cloud came a voice, "This is my beloved Son. Listen to him." Suddenly, looking around, they no longer saw anyone but Jesus alone with them.

As they were coming down from the mountain, he charged them not to relate what they had seen to anyone, except when the Son of Man had risen from the dead. So they kept the matter to themselves, questioning what rising from the dead meant.

MARK 9: 2-10

SAINT BENEDICT

"When someone comes first to the monastic life, he should not be allowed entry too readily, but as the Apostle says: 'Test whether the spirits be godly' [1 Jn 4:1]. Thus if the newcomer continues knocking and is seen to bear patiently for four or five days the rebuffs offered him and the difficulty of entrance, and if he persists in his request, then let him come in."

RB 58.1–4a

REFLECTION

As mysterious and frightening as was the apostles' experience on Mount Tabor when the Lord was transfigured before their eyes and Moses and Elijah appeared conversing with Jesus, yet still Peter could say, "Master, it is good that we are here." For the Christian, these words ought to be true no matter what the circumstances of our lives for as Christians we seek to do God's will. Wherever and whenever we are there are opportunities for us to share in the ministry of Christ in reconciling all things to God.

Saint Benedict legislates that an aspirant to the monastery ought to be made to knock at the door a few times to test his resolve, to see if this person is indeed ready to say, "It is good for me to be here." It is good for us to be in the season of Lent and it is good for us to undergo the discipline of Lent so that we might in grace live fully present to the Lord.

PRAYER

Heavenly Father, you offer to us right now at this very moment, right here where we are reading this prayer the occasion to be in your presence and to rejoice in our communion with you. Hear us as we call. May our response to your invitation be with hearts ready to serve you. We ask this in the name of Jesus the Lord. Amen.

GOSPEL

Jesus took Peter, John, and James and went up the mountain to pray. While he was praying his face changed in appearance and his clothing became dazzling white. And behold, two men were conversing with him, Moses and Elijah, who appeared in glory and spoke of his exodus that he was going to accomplish in Jerusalem. Peter and his companions had been overcome by sleep, but becoming fully awake, they saw his glory and the two men standing with him. As they were about to part from him, Peter said to Jesus, "Master, it is good that we are here; let us make three tents, one for you, one for Moses, and one for Elijah." But he did not know what he was saying. While he was still speaking, a cloud came and cast a shadow over them, and they became frightened when they entered the cloud. Then from the cloud came a voice that said, "This is my chosen Son; listen to him." After the voice had spoken, Jesus was found alone. They fell silent and did not at that time tell anyone what they had seen.

LUKE 9: 28B-36

SAINT BENEDICT

"It is the master's role to speak and teach; the disciple is to keep silent and listen."

RB 6.6

REFLECTION

Peter, James, and John became terrified at the sight of the Christ transfigured once they were fully awake to what was happening before their eyes. Peter stumbled in his speech to say something that would give meaning to the event and he spoke about erecting three tents or booths in honor of the three glorious figures before them, "but he did not know what he was saying." The voice from the cloud then spoke, and it was these words that gave meaning to the event and to what truly mattered most: "This is my chosen Son; listen to him."

For Saint Benedict a very important, indeed crucial, task for the monk is to learn how to listen to the beloved Son, the Word of God. The first lesson, then, is simply to be taught and to become practiced in being silent. Lent is a time for us to study silence. This silence or taciturnity is meant to help us to develop an eagerness to hear the Word, for in that Word is the revelation of God's love and purpose. This silence is a desire to allow the Word to be the measure of all the other words that surround us inside and out. This silence is the humble and joyful preparation to welcome into our hearts the Transfigured Christ.

PRAYER

God our Father, you revealed to the apostles the glory of your Son who came among us for the forgiveness of sins and the salvation of the world. As he sought only to do your will, may we during this Lent become more attentive to your Word that reveals your will for us and so be prepared to celebrate the glory of Christ's Resurrection. We make this prayer through Christ our Lord. Amen.

GOSPEL

JESUS SAID TO HIS DISCIPLES:

"Be merciful, just as your Father is merciful.

"Stop judging and you will not be judged. Stop condemning and you will not be condemned. Forgive and you will be forgiven. Give and gifts will be given to you; a good measure, packed together, shaken down, and overflowing, will be poured into your lap. For the measure with which you measure will in return be measured out to you."

LUKE 6: 36-38

SAINT BENEDICT

"He should be chaste, temperate and merciful, and always put mercy before judgment *[Jas 2:13] so that he himself may obtain the former. He should hate vices but love the brothers."*

RB 64.9b–11

REFLECTION

The abbot of a monastery, in Saint Benedict's vision, takes the place of Christ; he is the viceregent (*agere vices*) of Christ and therefore must act toward the members of the community in a manner that closely follows the ideal of Christ. In particular, Saint Benedict is keen to emphasize the quality of mercy. Partly this is the case because the abbot will have to give an account of his stewardship before the judgment seat of God. Partly this is the case because the divine law calls him to be compassionate "as [our] Father is compassionate." All of us are called in this season of Lent to be especially mindful of the words of the Lord spoken by the prophet Jeremiah: "I have loved you with an everlasting love" (Jer 31:3).

By meditating and acting on these words, may we attend carefully not only during Lent but all the days of our lives to our obligation and duty not simply not to judge and condemn, but rather generously, even extravagantly, to show mercy and compassion according to the measure of mercy and compassion shown to us by God.

PRAYER

Father of mercy, help us to confess and to do penance for our sins so that we may rejoice in the newness of life won for us by your son Jesus Christ, who is Lord forever and ever. Amen.

GOSPEL

Jesus spoke to the crowds and to his disciples, saying, "The scribes and the Pharisees have taken their seat on the chair of Moses. Therefore, do and observe all things whatsoever they tell you, but do not follow their example. For they preach but they do not practice. They tie up heavy burdens hard to carry and lay them on people's shoulders, but they will not lift a finger to move them. All their works are performed to be seen. They widen their phylacteries and lengthen their tassels. They love places of honor at banquets, seats of honor in synagogues, greetings in marketplaces, and the salutation 'Rabbi.' As for you, do not be called 'Rabbi.' You have but one teacher, and you are all brothers. Call no one on earth your father; you have but one Father in heaven. Do not be called 'Master'; you have but one master, the Christ. The greatest among you must be your servant. Whoever exalts himself will be humbled; but whoever humbles himself will be exalted."

MATTHEW 23: 1-12

SAINT BENEDICT

"Due to this love [for God], [the monk] can now begin to accomplish effortlessly, as if spontaneously, everything that he previously did out of fear. He will do this no longer out of fear of hell but out of love for Christ, good habit itself and a delight in virtue. Once his worker has been cleansed of vices and sins, the Lord will graciously make all this shine forth in him by the power of the Holy Spirit."

RB 7.68–70

REFLECTION

The seventh chapter of Saint Benedict's Rule is entitled "On Humility" and he opens it with a citation of Mt 23:12: "Whoever humbles himself shall be exalted, but whoever exalts himself shall be humbled." Saint Benedict then explains the twelve steps of humility through which the monk was to advance, beginning with a constant awareness of the awesome presence of God in his life and concluding with the monk's manifesting humility always in his heart and in his bearing: "Whether he is at the Work of God, in the oratory, in the monastery, in the garden, on a journey, in the field or anywhere at all, whether sitting, walking or standing" (RB 7.63). No easy path this growth in humility either for the monk or for anyone else. "But for God all things are possible" (Mt 19:26).

Therefore as we reflect during these first three weeks of Lent on Christ's call to us for conversion, penance, and reform, indeed his call for us to grow in humility as he himself was humble, we acknowledge our need for God's grace and we confidently turn to him to strengthen our resolve and to help us in our Lenten practices to give all glory to him.

PRAYER

Without you, Lord, we can do nothing and all our efforts would be for naught, for "unless the Lord build the house, in vain do the builders labor" (Ps 127:1). Hear our prayer, come to our aid; fill us with your love. You live and reign forever and ever. Amen.

GOSPEL

As Jesus was going up to Jerusalem, he took the Twelve disciples aside by themselves, and said to them on the way, "Behold, we are going up to Jerusalem, and the Son of Man will be handed over to the chief priests and the scribes, and they will condemn him to death, and hand him over to the Gentiles to be mocked and scourged and crucified, and he will be raised on the third day."

Then the mother of the sons of Zebedee approached Jesus with her sons and did him homage, wishing to ask him for something. He said to her, "What do you wish?" She answered him, "Command that these two sons of mine sit, one at your right and the other at your left, in your kingdom." Jesus said in reply, "You do not know what you are asking. Can you drink the chalice that I am going to drink?" They said to him, "We can." He replied, "My chalice you will indeed drink, but to sit at my right and at my left, this is not mine to give but is for those for whom it has been prepared by my Father." When the ten heard this, they became indignant at the two brothers. But Jesus summoned them and said, "You know that the rulers of the Gentiles lord it over them, and the great ones make their authority over them felt. But it shall not be so among you. Rather, whoever wishes to be great among you shall be your servant; whoever wishes to be first among you shall be your slave. Just so, the Son of Man did not come to be served but to serve and to give his life as a ransom for many."

MATTHEW 20: 17-28

SAINT BENEDICT

"A wise old monk should be stationed at the gate of the monastery. He should know how to listen to people and also how to speak to them; his age should prevent him from wandering about. . . . As soon as anyone knocks or a poor person cries out, he should respond 'Thanks be to God' or 'Bless me!'"

RB 66.1, 3–4

REFLECTION

If we truly desire to be disciples of Christ, we never stop serving. Many years ago, I was with a group of other juniors monks who had gone to a wake at a convent for the sister of one of the senior monks. As we were leaving, an elderly nun, red-faced and out of breath, caught up with us as we were leaving the convent. "Now just slow down!" she panted. "I'm too old to be chasing you youngsters out into the parking lot." She was the portress, the sister in charge of receiving guests and visitors to the convent, and she had been sent to fetch us by the superior who wanted us to stay for tea. Saint Benedict would gladly point to her as a model for the porter he described in chapter 66 of his Rule.

Today's Gospel challenges us in this season of Lent to consider our service to others in the light of Christ's teaching, manifested by the depth of our willingness to be one with those whom God sends into our lives and of our services to them offered in the Spirit of Jesus who gave himself for us even unto death on a cross.

PRAYER

Lead us, Lord, into a deeper following of your way so that we may come to see that only in following it will we be more completely united to you and experience the fullness of joy promised to those who serve your people faithfully and loving for your sake. In your holy name we pray. Amen.

GOSPEL

JESUS SAID TO THE PHARISEES:

"There was a rich man who dressed in purple garments and fine linen and dined sumptuously each day. And lying at his door was a poor man named Lazarus, covered with sores, who would gladly have eaten his fill of the scraps that fell from the rich man's table. Dogs even used to come and lick his sores. When the poor man died, he was carried away by angels to the bosom of Abraham. The rich man also died and was buried, and from the netherworld, where he was in torment, he raised his eyes and saw Abraham far off and Lazarus at his side. And he cried out, 'Father Abraham, have pity on me. Send Lazarus to dip the tip of his finger in water and cool my tongue, for I am suffering torment in these flames.' Abraham replied, 'My child, remember that you received what was good during your lifetime while Lazarus likewise received what was bad; but now he is comforted here, whereas you are tormented. Moreover, between us and you a great chasm is established to prevent anyone from crossing who might wish to go from our side to yours or from your side to ours.' He said, 'Then I beg you, father, send him to my father's house, for I have five brothers, so that he may warn them, lest they too come to this place of torment.' But Abraham replied, 'They have Moses and the prophets. Let them listen to them.' He said, 'Oh no, father Abraham, but if someone from the dead goes to them, they will repent.' Then Abraham said, 'If they will not listen to Moses and the prophets, neither will they be persuaded if someone should rise from the dead.'"

LUKE 16: 19-31

SAINT BENEDICT

"[The cellarer] should lavish great care on the sick, the children, the guests and the poor."

RB 31.9a

REFLECTION

Saint Benedict was very conscious of the poor. In his vision for the monastery, the community of monks, despite a lifestyle that would segregate them from the world for the sake of contemplating and glorifying God, had an obligation under divine justice to provide for the needs of the poor as best it could. Not only was the cellarer, the monastic official charged with stewardship of the monastery's goods and property, to "lavish great care" on the poor and not only was the porter at the gate to respond "Thanks be to God" when a poor person cried out (RB 66.3), but the entire community was to show solicitude for the poor in receiving them as guests (53.15) or in the distribution of clothing and other material needs (RB 55.9, 58.24). No one in the monastery was exempt from serving the poor.

Almsgiving is one of the three principle disciplines of Lent, along with fasting and prayer, counseled by Christ and urged by the Church. Each of us needs to find a way to do this in the spirit of Christ and to continue to do it throughout the year.

PRAYER

By means of the disciplines of Lent, O Lord, you form us as a people peculiarly your own to give witness to your love and compassion and mercy. Grant us the grace to fulfill our obligations to all those in need and to be for them a sign of your love. We ask this through Christ our Lord. Amen.

GOSPEL

JESUS SAID TO THE CHIEF PRIESTS AND THE ELDERS OF THE PEOPLE:

"Hear another parable. There was a landowner who planted a vineyard, put a hedge around it, dug a wine press in it, and built a tower. Then he leased it to tenants and went on a journey. When vintage time drew near, he sent his servants to the tenants to obtain his produce. But the tenants seized the servants and one they beat, another they killed, and a third they stoned. Again he sent other servants, more numerous than the first ones, but they treated them in the same way. Finally, he sent his son to them, thinking, 'They will respect my son.' But when the tenants saw the son, they said to one another, 'This is the heir. Come, let us kill him and acquire his inheritance.' They seized him, threw him out of the vineyard, and killed him. What will the owner of the vineyard do to those tenants when he comes?" They answered him, "He will put those wretched men to a wretched death and lease his vineyard to other tenants who will give him the produce at the proper times." Jesus said to them, "Did you never read in the Scriptures:

The stone that the builders rejected
has become the cornerstone;
by the Lord has this been done,
and it is wonderful in our eyes?

Therefore, I say to you, the Kingdom of God will be taken away from you and given to a people that will produce its fruit."

When the chief priests and the Pharisees heard his parables, they knew that he was speaking about them. And although they were attempting to arrest him, they feared the crowds, for they regarded him as a prophet.

MATTHEW 21: 33-43, 45-46

SAINT BENEDICT

"The third step of humility is to submit to the superior in all obedience for love of God. In this, we imitate the Lord, of whom the Apostle says: He became obedient to the point of death."

RB 7.34

REFLECTION

The mission of Christ, who is one in being with the Father and who was sent by the Father, is a mission of sacrifice and redemption stemming from love: "God's love was revealed in our midst in this way: he sent his only Son to the world that we might have life through him. Love, then, consists in this: not that we have loved God, but that he has loved us and has sent his Son as an offering for our sins" (1 Jn 4:9–10). It is this love, this identification with the mission of Christ to which we are called: "Beloved, if God has loved us so, we must have the same love for one another" (1 Jn 4:11). But here's the rub: just as the love of Christ included those very Pharisees who sought first to ridicule and mock him and then later who worked to secure his humiliation and death, so must we extend our love unilaterally to all.

In my monastery the third step of humility from Saint Benedict's Rule is read at the conclusion of the meals on Good Friday and Holy Saturday, a clear reminder of what Lent and Holy Week are really all about. The reading offers us and our guests the opportunity to reflect honestly on our understanding of our own mission and purpose in the light of Christ's mission and to heed the counsel of Saint Benedict that all we do be done "for love of God."

PRAYER

Lord God, you continually call us out of darkness into your own marvelous light. May we confess our sins when we fail to act in love and may we grow in that humility and compassion witnessed by your son, Jesus Christ our Lord, in whose name we pray. Amen.

GOSPEL

Tax collectors and sinners were all drawing near to listen to Jesus, but the Pharisees and scribes began to complain, saying, "This man welcomes sinners and eats with them." So to them Jesus addressed this parable. "A man had two sons, and the younger son said to his father, 'Father, give me the share of your estate that should come to me.' So the father divided the property between them. After a few days, the younger son collected all his belongings and set off to a distant country where he squandered his inheritance on a life of dissipation. When he had freely spent everything, a severe famine struck that country, and he found himself in dire need. So he hired himself out to one of the local citizens who sent him to his farm to tend the swine. And he longed to eat his fill of the pods on which the swine fed, but nobody gave him any. Coming to his senses he thought, 'How many of my father's hired workers have more than enough food to eat, but here am I, dying from hunger. I shall get up and go to my father and I shall say to him, "Father, I have sinned against heaven and against you. I no longer deserve to be called your son; treat me as you would treat one of your hired workers."' So he got up and went back to his father. While he was still a long way off, his father caught sight of him, and was filled with compassion. He ran to his son, embraced him and kissed him. His son said to him, 'Father, I have sinned against heaven and against you; I no longer deserve to be called your son.' But his father ordered his servants, 'Quickly, bring the finest robe and put it on him; put a ring on his finger and sandals on his feet. Take the fattened calf and slaughter it. Then let us celebrate with a feast, because this son of mine was dead, and has come to life again; he was lost, and has been found.' Then the celebration began. Now the older son had been out in the field and, on his way back, as he neared the house, he heard the sound of music and dancing. He called one of the servants and asked what this might mean. The servant said to him, 'Your brother has returned and your father has slaughtered the fattened calf because he has him back safe and sound.' He became angry, and when he refused to enter the house, his father came out and pleaded with him. He said to his father in reply, 'Look, all these years I served you and not once did I disobey your orders; yet you never gave me even a young goat to feast on with my friends. But when your son returns who swallowed up your property with prostitutes, for him you slaughter the fattened calf.' He said to him, 'My son, you are here with me always; everything I have is yours. But now we must celebrate and rejoice, because your brother was dead and has come to life again; he was lost and has been found.'"

LUKE 15: 1-3, 11-32

SAINT BENEDICT

"The abbot must indeed exercise very great care, and hasten with all keenness and energy to prevent any of the sheep in his care from being lost. He should understand that he has undertaken to care for the weak and not to dominate the strong."

RB 27.5–6

REFLECTION

According to the mind of Saint Benedict, the abbot is to assume the role of the father in the Parable of the Prodigal Son. Like a wise physician, he is to use all the skills he commands as well as the assistance of wise and experienced monks to reach out to those who have violated the Rule, who have been disobedient to his orders, or who have fallen under the terrible weight of temptation. And when all else fails in his store of remedies, the abbot is to invoke the most powerful medicine of them all: "And if he sees that his efforts have accomplished nothing, let him try a still greater thing: he and all the brothers should pray that the Lord, who can do all things, will heal the troubled brother" (RB 28.4–5).

Only when we realize our need for conversion are we truly ready for reconciliation, for what Pope John Paul II called "the father's festive and loving welcome." Lent invites us not only to seek genuine conversion and reconciliation, but also to become instruments of healing and renewal in others.

PRAYER

Heavenly Father, help us to reject the temptation to build a world for ourselves and instead to embrace your will and your love. May Christ who suffered and died for us lead us into your kingdom of justice and peace. Grant this through Christ our Lord. Amen.

THIRD WEEK
OF
LENT

GOSPEL

Jesus came to a town of Samaria called Sychar, near the plot of land that Jacob had given to his son Joseph. Jacob's well was there. Jesus, tired from his journey, sat down there at the well. It was about noon.

A woman of Samaria came to draw water. Jesus said to her, "Give me a drink." His disciples had gone into the town to buy food. The Samaritan woman said to him, "How can you, a Jew, ask me, a Samaritan woman, for a drink?" — For Jews use nothing in common with Samaritans. — Jesus answered and said to her, "If you knew the gift of God and who is saying to you, 'Give me a drink,' you would have asked him and he would have given you living water." The woman said to him, "Sir, you do not even have a bucket and the cistern is deep; where then can you get this living water? Are you greater than our father Jacob, who gave us this cistern and drank from it himself with his children and his flocks?" Jesus answered and said to her, "Everyone who drinks this water will be thirsty again; but whoever drinks the water I shall give will never thirst; the water I shall give will become in him a spring of water welling up to eternal life." The woman said to him, "Sir, give me this water, so that I may not be thirsty or have to keep coming here to draw water."

Jesus said to her, "Go call your husband and come back." The woman answered and said to him, "I do not have a husband." Jesus answered her, "You are right in saying, 'I do not have a husband.' For you have had five husbands, and the one you have now is not your husband. What you have said is true." The woman said to him, "Sir, I can see that you are a prophet. Our ancestors worshiped on this mountain; but you people say that the place to worship is in Jerusalem." Jesus said to her, "Believe me, woman, the hour is coming when you will worship the Father neither on this mountain nor in Jerusalem. You people worship what you do not understand; we worship what we understand, because salvation is from the Jews. But the hour is coming, and is now here, when true worshipers will worship the Father in Spirit and truth; and indeed the

Father seeks such people to worship him. God is Spirit, and those who worship him must worship in Spirit and truth." The woman said to him, "I know that the Messiah is coming, the one called the Christ; when he comes, he will tell us everything." Jesus said to her, "I am he, the one speaking with you."

At that moment his disciples returned, and were amazed that he was talking with a woman, but still no one said, "What are you looking for?" or "Why are you talking with her?" The woman left her water jar and went into the town and said to the people, "Come see a man who told me everything I have done. Could he possibly be the Christ?" They went out of the town and came to him. Meanwhile, the disciples urged him, "Rabbi, eat." But he said to them, "I have food to eat of which you do not know." So the disciples said to one another, "Could someone have brought him something to eat?" Jesus said to them, "My food is to do the will of the one who sent me and to finish his work. Do you not say, 'In four months the harvest will be here'? I tell you, look up and see the fields ripe for the harvest. The reaper is already receiving payment and gathering crops for eternal life, so that the sower and reaper can rejoice together. For here the saying is verified that 'One sows and another reaps.' I sent you to reap what you have not worked for; others have done the work, and you are sharing the fruits of their work."

Many of the Samaritans of that town began to believe in him because of the word of the woman who testified, "He told me everything I have done." When the Samaritans came to him, they invited him to stay with them; and he stayed there two days. Many more began to believe in him because of his word, and they said to the woman, "We no longer believe because of your word; for we have heard for ourselves, and we know that this is truly the savior of the world."

JOHN 4: 5-42

Shorter form: JOHN 4:5-15, 19b-26, 39a, 40-42
Longer form may be optionally read on any day in the third week of Lent

SAINT BENEDICT

"They must show selfless love to the brothers. Let them fear God out of love. They should love their abbot with sincere and humble charity. Let them prefer absolutely nothing to Christ, and may he lead us all together to everlasting life."

RB 72.8–12

REFLECTION

Jesus is the wellspring, the font, the water of eternal life. He offers to each of us created in the image and likeness of God the hope of having all our spiritual desires fulfilled when our hearts live in his love. But our love must be God-centered, genuine, and sacrificial if the water of eternal life is going to be effective in us, as the Samaritan woman discovered when she encountered Jesus at the well. Saint Benedict is very insistent on a monk's growth in and practice of love toward all: God, the abbot, the brothers. In his Rule, Saint Benedict emphasizes this by using several Latin terms for love, each with a distinctive meaning, so that the core reality of love will not be missed by anyone reading it.

It would be somewhat odd and perhaps a bit facetious to say, "Lent is for lovers," but for those who have penetrated into the deep meaning and significance of this holy season and of Eastertide, there is really nothing else than love.

PRAYER

Lord Jesus, you welcome all to the water of eternal life. Hear our prayer for those who do not yet know of your infinite love for them, that one day they may taste and see the goodness of the Lord. You live and reign forever and ever. Amen.

GOSPEL

Since the Passover of the Jews was near, Jesus went up to Jerusalem. He found in the temple area those who had sold oxen, sheep and doves, as well as the money changers seated there. He made a whip out of cords and drove them all out of the temple area, with sheep and oxen, and spilled the coins of the money changers and overturned their tables, and to those who sold doves he said, "Take these out of here, and stop making my Father's house a marketplace." His disciples recalled the words of Scripture, *Zeal for your house will consume me.* At this the Jews answered and said to him, "What sign can you show us for doing this?" Jesus answered and said to them, "Destroy this temple and in three days I will raise it up." The Jews said, "This temple has been under construction for forty-six years, and you will raise it up in three days?" But he was speaking about the temple of his body. Therefore, when he was raised from the dead, his disciples remembered that he had said this, and they came to believe the Scripture and the word Jesus had spoken.

While he was in Jerusalem for the feast of Passover, many began to believe in his name when they saw the signs he was doing. But Jesus would not trust himself to them because he knew them all, and did not need anyone to testify about human nature. He himself understood it well.

JOHN 2: 13-25

SAINT BENEDICT

"The oratory should be in fact what it is called, and nothing else should be done or stored there. When the Work of God is finished, they should all leave in deepest silence and show reverence for God. . . . If someone perhaps wishes to pray privately at some other time, let him simply go in and pray, not in a loud voice but with tears and full attention of heart."

RB 52.1–2, 4

REFLECTION

Saint Benedict's remarks about the physical layout of the monastery are rather succinct. He simply lists what should be within the cloister so that the monks do not have to go outside to obtain what is necessary: water, mill, garden, workshops, etc. The one special place which receives attention is the chapel or oratory. It is there that the monks spend a significant portion of the day offering praise and thanks to God in the eight daily gatherings for the recitation of the Divine Office. Therefore, as Saint Benedict clearly states, "nothing else should be done or stored there" not only because of the regular communal prayer that takes place in it but also because a monk should feel welcome to enter there and pray in private, humbly acknowledging his sins and quietly contemplating the loving presence of God in his life.

Each Christian soul is a temple of the Holy Spirit. Therefore nothing sinful should be kept there or entertained there or stored there. Our efforts, especially during Lent, should be to cleanse ourselves through the disciplines of prayer, fasting, and almsgiving so that we might be more worthy to enter into the sacred mysteries of Christ's passion, death, and Resurrection.

PRAYER

God our Father in heaven, hear the prayers of your people who call out to you in prayer. May we serve you humbly and faithfully during this season of Lent and so come with joy and holy longing to the feast of Easter with hearts cleansed and renewed. We make this prayer through Christ our Lord. Amen.

GOSPEL

Some people told Jesus about the Galileans whose blood Pilate had mingled with the blood of their sacrifices. Jesus said to them in reply, "Do you think that because these Galileans suffered in this way they were greater sinners than all other Galileans? By no means! But I tell you, if you do not repent, you will all perish as they did! Or those eighteen people who were killed when the tower at Siloam fell on them – do you think they were more guilty than everyone else who lived in Jerusalem? By no means! But I tell you, if you do not repent, you will all perish as they did!"

And he told them this parable: "There once was a person who had a fig tree planted in his orchard, and when he came in search of fruit on it but found none, he said to the gardener, 'For three years now I have come in search of fruit on this fig tree but have found none. So cut it down. Why should it exhaust the soil? "He said to him in reply, 'Sir, leave it for this year also, and I shall cultivate the ground around it and fertilize it; it may bear fruit in the future. If not you can cut it down.'"

LUKE 13: 1-9

SAINT BENEDICT

"A brother who is judged guilty of a more serious fault should be excluded from both table and oratory. No brother is to associate or converse with him in any fashion. Let him work alone at what he is told to do."

RB 25.1–3a

REFLECTION

Saint Benedict does not want to punish monks for constant complaining, for failing to fulfill tasks assigned to them in obedience, or for acting in ways that are contrary to the Rule. Rather he desires that a monk guilty of any offense be willing to admit his fault and make satisfaction. Only if the monk refuses to do this does Saint Benedict invoke the strictures of punishment, whose purpose again is to elicit from the monk repentance and conversion. The purpose of the strictures can be understood as a way to make the monk realize the isolation that sin and recalcitrance entail. As quickly as possible would Saint Benedict reincorporate a wayward monk back into the communal life, but that can happen only when the monk by the grace of God confesses and makes proper reparation in humility.

The Scripture readings for Lent, especially during the first three weeks, invite us to give serious consideration to our sinful behavior. The Lord desires to "cultivate" our lives, as it were, so that we might bear good fruit in abundance, but we must turn to him in humility and, acknowledging our sins, resolve with his grace to confess our sins, do penance, and reform our lives.

PRAYER

Time and again, Lord God, you call us to conversion by your freely given grace and you wait patiently for us to repent and reform our lives. Hear our prayer for mercy and grant us the will to turn to you and believe in the Good News of our salvation. We ask this through Christ our Lord. Amen.

GOSPEL

Jesus said to the people in the synagogue at Nazareth:

"Amen, I say to you, no prophet is accepted in his own native place. Indeed, I tell you, there were many widows in Israel in the days of Elijah when the sky was closed for three and a half years and a severe famine spread over the entire land. It was to none of these that Elijah was sent, but only to a widow in Zarephath in the land of Sidon. Again, there were many lepers in Israel during the time of Elisha the prophet; yet not one of them was cleansed, but only Naaman the Syrian." When the people in the synagogue heard this, they were all filled with fury. They rose up, drove him out of the town, and led him to the brow of the hill on which their town had been built, to hurl him down headlong. But he passed through the midst of them and went away.

LUKE 4: 24-30

SAINT BENEDICT

"Therefore, if you long to attain the heavenly homeland, with Christ's assistance carry out this modest Rule for beginners that we have sketched out. Only then will you arrive with God's protection at the higher peaks of doctrine and virtue that we have pointed out. Amen."

RB 73.8–9

REFLECTION

One of the senior monks in our community was always the first to arrive in the chapel for the Divine Office or for Mass, in spite of ongoing illness and disabilities. In speaking with him one time, I mentioned this admirable trait. He responded with a shy smile and quiet voice, "Well, I wouldn't want anyone to think I had anything better to do." Such total commitment to the service of God and to the life he had chosen in his continuing effort to live up to the vows he had made so many years before as a young man revealed what he would in fact have probably denied: that he was no longer a beginner in the spiritual life and that, like Jesus and the prophets of the Old Testament, he was prepared in any circumstance or trial or difficulty or danger to give witness to God.

In Lent, the reality of Christ's total commitment to our redemption is made manifest. May we in turn renew and revitalize our commitment to him in the grace of this season.

PRAYER

Cleanse your people, O Lord, of all their sins and impurities that they may give witness to you in good times and in bad, in sickness and in health, whether richer or poorer, that in all things God may be glorified. You live and reign forever and ever. Amen.

GOSPEL

Peter approached Jesus and asked him, "Lord, if my brother sins against me, how often must I forgive him? As many as seven times?" Jesus answered, "I say to you, not seven times but seventy-seven times. That is why the Kingdom of heaven may be likened to a king who decided to settle accounts with his servants. When he began the accounting, a debtor was brought before him who owed him a huge amount. Since he had no way of paying it back, his master ordered him to be sold, along with his wife, his children, and all his property, in payment of the debt. At that, the servant fell down, did him homage, and said, 'Be patient with me, and I will pay you back in full.' Moved with compassion the master of that servant let him go and forgave him the loan. When that servant had left, he found one of his fellow servants who owed him a much smaller amount. He seized him and started to choke him, demanding, 'Pay back what you owe.' Falling to his knees, his fellow servant begged him, 'Be patient with me, and I will pay you back.' But he refused. Instead, he had him put in prison until he paid back the debt. Now when his fellow servants saw what had happened, they were deeply disturbed, and went to their master and reported the whole affair. His master summoned him and said to him, 'You wicked servant! I forgave you your entire debt because you begged me to. Should you not have had pity on your fellow servant, as I had pity on you?' Then in anger his master handed him over to the torturers until he should pay back the whole debt. So will my heavenly Father do to you, unless each of you forgives your brother from your heart."

MATTHEW 18: 21-35

SAINT BENEDICT

"If, however, it is a question of a hidden problem of conscience, [the monk] should only reveal it to the abbot or one of the spiritual seniors. For they should know how to cure their own wounds and those of others, without divulging them in public."

RB 46.5–6

REFLECTION

Saint Benedict wanted his monks to develop the habit of forgiveness. He urged them to make satisfaction for any faults or failings that they may have been committed in the presence of others: damage to tools or other monastery property, errors in the recitation of the Divine Office, grumbling or complaining to others about one's situation. He further said that sins or hidden problems of the conscience should be revealed to a spiritual father who can offer guidance and counsel and forgiveness. In these matters, Saint Benedict was not being picky, but he was expressing his understanding that the need for forgiveness is an ongoing reality and that the monks best dispose themselves to forgive others when they know the peace of being forgiven.

The commandment to forgive seven times seventy times is one of the most radical and demanding of the commandments given by Christ in the Gospels. To help us develop the habit of forgiveness so that we can fulfill this commandment, the Church calls us in a special way during Lent to seek forgiveness in the Sacrament of Reconciliation and then to forgive as we have been forgiven.

PRAYER

Good and gracious God, you reveal your plan of salvation in the teachings of your Son, Jesus Christ. Grant us the grace to give ear to what he says and so put his words into action in our lives. We make this prayer through Christ our Lord. Amen.

GOSPEL

JESUS SAID TO HIS DISCIPLES:

"Do not think that I have come to abolish the law or the prophets. I have come not to abolish but to fulfill. Amen, I say to you, until heaven and earth pass away, not the smallest letter or the smallest part of a letter will pass from the law, until all things have taken place. Therefore, whoever breaks one of the least of these commandments and teaches others to do so will be called least in the Kingdom of heaven. But whoever obeys and teaches these commandments will be called greatest in the Kingdom of heaven."

MATTHEW 5: 17-19

SAINT BENEDICT

"At Sunday Prime, four sections of Psalm 118 are to be sung. At the remaining hours, that is, Terce, Sext and None, three sections of the aforesaid Psalm 118 should be sung. . . . At Terce, Sext and None of Monday, the nine parts of Psalm 118 which remain, three at each hour. Thus Psalm 118 will be used up in two days, that is, Sunday and Monday. . . . And so Psalm 118 will always begin on Sunday."

RB 18.2–3, 7–8, 11

REFLECTION

In his precise ordering of the recitation of the psalms for the Divine Office (RB 8–18), Saint Benedict is particularly concerned that Psalm 118 be recited in its entirety. This psalm is a great hymn of praise of God's law. It is written in the style of the Old Testament Wisdom Literature like Proverbs, Wisdom, and Sirach. It invites those praying it to consider how wonderful it is that God has revealed his law to us, a law that does not intend so much to restrict human behavior as to help us give meaning to our lives by understanding the mysterious working of God's love. This psalm offers us words "of spirit and life" which are the source of the moral force in any human law and which help us to become mature Christians prepared for the joys of the Kingdom of Heaven. Saint Benedict desires that Psalm 118 be recited at the very beginning of the week so that its beauty and its theme might assist the monks as their week unfolds to live according to the will of God for them more closely.

Jesus teaches us in today's Gospel that "not the smallest part of a letter" of God's law will pass away. In Lent we are called to embrace in love the law of God revealed in love.

PRAYER

Draw us ever closer to you, Lord, that by the observance of your law we may unite our Lenten sacrifices to the great sacrifice you offered for the forgiveness of our sins and the salvation of our souls. You live and reign forever and ever. Amen.

GOSPEL

Jesus was driving out a demon that was mute, and when the demon had gone out, the mute man spoke and the crowds were amazed. Some of them said, "By the power of Beelzebul, the prince of demons, he drives out demons." Others, to test him, asked him for a sign from heaven. But he knew their thoughts and said to them, "Every kingdom divided against itself will be laid waste and house will fall against house. And if Satan is divided against himself, how will his kingdom stand? For you say that it is by Beelzebul that I drive out demons. If I, then, drive out demons by Beelzebul, by whom do your own people drive them out? Therefore they will be your judges. But if it is by the finger of God that I drive out demons, then the Kingdom of God has come upon you. When a strong man fully armed guards his palace, his possessions are safe. But when one stronger than he attacks and overcomes him, he takes away the armor on which he relied and distributes the spoils. Whoever is not with me is against me, and whoever does not gather with me scatters."

LUKE 11: 14-23

SAINT BENEDICT

"The fourth step of humility is this: when obedience involves harsh, hostile things or even injustice of some sort, one embraces them patiently with no outcry. Let us bear such things without flagging or fleeing, as Scripture says: Whoever perseveres to the end will be saved."

RB 7.35–36

REFLECTION

Our vocation as Christians, from the day of our baptism, is to engage in our call to "gather" with Christ. Our vocation is to know that, by the grace of God and the power of the Sacraments, we are on the path of redemption. This path is the Way that leads to life eternal. It is never an easy one: Jesus himself said, "How narrow the gate and constricted the road that leads to life. And those who find it are few" (Mt 7:14). It is the way of the cross, a way that, as Saint Benedict warns his disciples, can have "harsh, hostile things or even injustice of some sort." Yet by being faithful to Christ by walking in this way, we are gathered to Christ. Further, our vocation as Christians demands of us that we cease from "scattering," that is, that we turn away from sin and the lure of the devil, confident that Christ can drive him from us by the finger of God.

Lent calls us to renew and respond robustly to our vocation in Christ: never to scatter from him, always to gather with him. Thus we share, too, in his ministry of proclaiming the Good News to all the world.

PRAYER

Help us, O God, to remain true to the discipline of Lent that we might share more fully in your abundant love and celebrate with joy the Paschal Mystery of your son, Jesus the Christ, who is Lord forever and ever. Amen.

GOSPEL

One of the scribes came to Jesus and asked him, "Which is the first of all the commandments?" Jesus replied, "The first is this: *Hear, O Israel! The Lord our God is Lord alone! You shall love the Lord your God with all your heart, with all your soul, with all your mind, and with all your strength.* The second is this: *You shall love your neighbor as yourself.* There is no other commandment greater than these." The scribe said to him, "Well said, teacher. You are right in saying, *He is One and there is no other than he. And to love him with all your heart, with all your understanding, with all your strength, and to love your neighbor as yourself* is worth more than all burnt offerings and sacrifices." And when Jesus saw that he answered with understanding, he said to him, "You are not far from the Kingdom of God."

And no one dared to ask him any more questions.

MARK 12: 28-34

SAINT BENEDICT

"First, to love the Lord God with all your heart, all your soul and all your strength, then, your neighbor as yourself."

RB 4.1–2

REFLECTION

In chapter 4 of his Rule, Saint Benedict sets out a long series of commandments, maxims, and aphorisms drawn from a variety of Christian sources and intended to assist the monks to incarnate in their day-to-day living of the monastic life the principles and virtues of the Gospels. At the head of his list, in the first place (*in primis*) is the greatest commandment which Jesus gave in response to the question of the scribe: to love God and neighbor with all of one's being. But this is no easy commandment, for we, though baptized into Christ, yet remain broken in our nature because of sin. How can we love as we are commanded when we are so in need of healing? Only the grace of God can bring this about. God alone can restore us to that wholeness and fullness of being that enables us to love unreservedly and unselfishly in imitation of the sacrificial love of Christ. We are called upon in this great commandment to embrace God's love for us so that we might love as he has taught.

In the first place, then, Lent is about love, for the very purpose and the meaning of all Lenten penitential practices and disciplines are found in loving God and neighbor. In Lent, then, we are invited to participate ever more fully in the beauty of God's love.

PRAYER

You have revealed your love for us, O God our Father, throughout the ages and you have brought this revelation to its fullness in your son, Jesus Christ. In him you open for us the true way to return to you and to love you as you have loved us. May we always put in the first place the love taught to us by Christ who loved us to the end. We pray in his name. Amen.

GOSPEL

Jesus addressed this parable to those who were convinced of their own righteousness and despised everyone else. "Two people went up to the temple area to pray; one was a Pharisee and the other was a tax collector. The Pharisee took up his position and spoke this prayer to himself, 'O God, I thank you that I am not like the rest of humanity—greedy, dishonest, adulterous—or even like this tax collector. I fast twice a week, and I pay tithes on my whole income.' But the tax collector stood off at a distance and would not even raise his eyes to heaven but beat his breast and prayed, 'O God, be merciful to me a sinner.' I tell you, the latter went home justified, not the former; for everyone who exalts himself will be humbled, and the one who humbles himself will be exalted."

LUKE 18: 9-14

SAINT BENEDICT

"Constantly aware of his guilt for sins, he should consider himself to be already standing before the terrifying judgment of God. He should always repeat in his heart what the publican said in the gospel, his eyes cast downward: Lord, I am a sinner and not worthy to raise my eyes to heaven."

RB 7.64–65

REFLECTION

The Lord speaks directly to us in the words of the prophet Hosea and says, "It is mercy I desire, and not sacrifice" (Hos 6:6). No command could be more simple: be merciful. That's all: be merciful. And yet how hard it is, at times even seemingly impossible, for us to muster the energy, the humility, and the courage to be merciful. It is not necessarily that we see ourselves as better or worthier than another, although that is the great danger against which today's Gospel warns. It is more that we do not see the justice, the fairness in being merciful; we have the feeling that someone is being all too easily "let off the hook," so to speak, and that forgiveness and mercy are due only to those who are sincerely repentant and ready to make amends. But that is not for us to judge. Rather in spite of our misgivings, it is mercy that God asks of us, even demands of us, a sincere and genuine mercy with no conditions or strings attached. What a great grace it would be for us to be merciful like that, for to be that way is to be like God.

Saint Benedict, in his beautiful chapter "On Humility," realized the necessity of humility in one who would fulfill this call of God for mercy. In Lent we have an opportunity to make "being merciful" an object of our earnest prayer and commitment.

PRAYER

Father of mercies, you invite us into your presence and ask us to show to others the mercy you freely and graciously have shown to us in Christ Jesus. Grant us now and always the grace to be merciful and so to live in Spirit and in truth as your daughters and sons. We make this prayer through Christ our Lord. Amen.

FOURTH WEEK
OF
LENT

GOSPEL

As Jesus passed by he saw a man blind from birth. His disciples asked him, "Rabbi, who sinned, this man or his parents, that he was born blind?" Jesus answered, "Neither he nor his parents sinned; it is so that the works of God might be made visible through him. We have to do the works of the one who sent me while it is day. Night is coming when no one can work. While I am in the world, I am the light of the world." When he had said this, he spat on the ground and made clay with the saliva, and smeared the clay on his eyes, and said to him, "Go wash in the Pool of Siloam" —which means Sent. So he went and washed, and came back able to see.

His neighbors and those who had seen him earlier as a beggar said, "Isn't this the one who used to sit and beg?" Some said, "It is," but others said, "No, he just looks like him." He said, "I am." So they said to him, "How were your eyes opened?" He replied, "The man called Jesus made clay and anointed my eyes and told me, 'Go to Siloam and wash.' So I went there and washed and was able to see." And they said to him, "Where is he?" He said, "I don't know."

They brought the one who was once blind to the Pharisees. Now Jesus had made clay and opened his eyes on a sabbath. So then the Pharisees also asked him how he was able to see. He said to them, "He put clay on my eyes, and I washed, and now I can see." So some of the Pharisees said, "This man is not from God, because he does not keep the sabbath." But others said, "How can a sinful man do such signs?" And there was a division among them. So they said to the blind man again, "What do you have to say about him, since he opened your eyes?" He said, "He is a prophet."

Now the Jews did not believe that he had been blind and gained his sight until they summoned the parents of the one who had gained his sight. They asked them, "Is this your son, who you say was born blind? How does he now see?" His parents answered and said, "We know that this is our son and that he was born blind. We do not know how he sees now, nor do we know who opened his eyes. Ask him, he is of age; he can speak for himself." His parents said this because they were afraid of the Jews, for the Jews had already agreed that if anyone acknowledged him as the Christ, he would be expelled from the synagogue. For this reason his parents said, "He is of age; question him."

So a second time they called the man who had been blind and said to him, "Give God the praise! We know that this man is a sinner." He replied, "If he is a sinner, I do not know. One thing I do know is that I was blind and now I see." So they said to him, "What did he do to you? How did he open your eyes?" He answered them, "I told you already and you did not listen. Why do you want to hear it again? Do you want to become his disciples, too?" They ridiculed him and said, "You are that man's disciple; we are disciples of Moses! We know that God spoke to Moses, but we do not know where this one is from." The man answered and said to them, "This is what is so amazing, that you do not know where he is from, yet he opened my eyes. We know that God does not listen to sinners, but if one is devout and does his will, he listens to him. It is unheard of that anyone ever opened the eyes of a person born blind. If this man were not from God, he would not be able to do anything." They answered and said to him, "You were born totally in sin, and are you trying to teach us?" Then they threw him out.

When Jesus heard that they had thrown him out, he found him and said, "Do you believe in the Son of Man?" He answered and said, "Who is he, sir, that I may believe in him?" Jesus said to him, "You have seen him, the one speaking with you is he." He said, "I do believe, Lord," and he worshiped him. Then Jesus said, "I came into this world for judgment, so that those who do not see might see, and those who do see might become blind."

Some of the Pharisees who were with him heard this and said to him, "Surely we are not also blind, are we?" Jesus said to them, "If you were blind, you would have no sin; but now you are saying, 'We see,' so your sin remains."

JOHN 9: 1-41

Shorter form: JOHN 9:1, 6-9, 13-17, 34-38
Longer form may be optionally read on any day in the fourth week of Lent

SAINT BENEDICT

"Let us open our eyes to the divine light."

RB PROLOGUE 9a

REFLECTION

This Fourth Sunday of Lent is traditionally called Laetáre Sunday, a title taken from the opening words of the Entrance Antiphon of the Mass: "Laetáre, Ierúsalem" (Rejoice, Jerusalem). It is the middle Sunday of Lent and we look forward expectantly with joyful hearts to the coming feast of Easter. It is also a time of year when the light of the sun shines a bit longer each day. Thus this Sunday is a reminder to us of the Easter light, which is Christ and whose presence will soon be magnificently symbolized in the great Paschal Candle, a sign that we all draw our light and our sight from the radiant and powerful love of the Godhead.

In the Prologue of his Rule, Saint Benedict urged on those who wish to follow Christ: "Let us rise at long last. . . . Let us open our eyes to the divine light" (RB Prol. 8a, 9a). He pleaded with the monks not to hesitate but to respond without delay to the call of Christ: "We must run and accomplish now what will profit us for eternity" (RB Prol. 44). The light of Christ has been given to us and it beckons us to holiness and to spiritual peace. On this Rejoicing Sunday, let us respond to his call, as did the blind man in the Gospel, with faith and trust and in steadfast love: "Light of Christ! Thanks be to God!"

PRAYER

Lord Jesus Christ, you healed man born blind because he believed in you. Increase our faith, that we might serve you with ever greater devotion and help others to see the wonders of your love. You live and reign forever and ever. Amen.

GOSPEL

JESUS SAID TO NICODEMUS:

"Just as Moses lifted up the serpent in the desert, so must the Son of Man be lifted up, so that everyone who believes in him may have eternal life."

For God so loved the world that he gave his only Son, so that everyone who believes in him might not perish but might have eternal life. For God did not send his Son into the world to condemn the world, but that the world might be saved through him. Whoever believes in him will not be condemned, but whoever does not believe has already been condemned, because he has not believed in the name of the only Son of God. And this is the verdict, that the light came into the world, but people preferred darkness to light, because their works were evil. For everyone who does wicked things hates the light and does not come toward the light, so that his works might not be exposed. But whoever lives the truth comes to the light, so that his works may be clearly seen as done in God.

JOHN 3: 14-21

SAINT BENEDICT

"Speak the truth both in your heart and with your mouth."

RB 4.28

REFLECTION

No matter what walk of life one is living, there are always places to hide the truth. Saint Benedict understood that this is the case also for those who choose the monastic life. Thus one of the tools of good works he sets out in chapter 4 calls the monks to truthfulness and candor, especially as they seek God in conversion. That is, the monks need to recognize and acknowledge not only their shortcomings and failings in the day to day living of the life, but also the truth of their sinful condition. Thus while they are to make satisfaction for the mistakes they make in the presence of others, they are also to seek counsel and ask forgiveness for sins of their conscience from the wise, senior monks of the community, those learned in the divine law who have found their redemption in Christ alone. For only in Christ, raised up on the cross, can restoration and healing be obtained.

Nicodemus came to Jesus at night, but Jesus invited him into the light and truth of his mission. May this Lenten journey with Jesus and Saint Benedict help us to look to Jesus, the source and foundation of our faith, and to find in him alone the way to salvation.

PRAYER

Lord Jesus Christ, you promised eternal life to all who put their faith in you. As we celebrate with joy this Laetáre Sunday, may we renew our commitment to be faithful to the discipline of Lent and to the proclamation of your love to all people. You live and reign forever and ever. Amen.

GOSPEL

Tax collectors and sinners were all drawing near to listen to Jesus, but the Pharisees and scribes began to complain, saying, "This man welcomes sinners and eats with them."

So to them Jesus addressed this parable: "A man had two sons, and the younger son said to his father, 'Father, give me the share of your estate that should come to me.' So the father divided the property between them. After a few days, the younger son collected all his belongings and set off to a distant country where he squandered his inheritance on a life of dissipation. When he had freely spent everything, a severe famine struck that country, and he found himself in dire need. So he hired himself out to one of the local citizens who sent him to his farm to tend the swine. And he longed to eat his fill of the pods on which the swine fed, but nobody gave him any. Coming to his senses he thought, 'How many of my father's hired workers have more than enough food to eat, but here am I, dying from hunger. I shall get up and go to my father and I shall say to him, "Father, I have sinned against heaven and against you. I no longer deserve to be called your son; treat me as you would treat one of your hired workers."' So he got up and went back to his father. While he was still a long way off, his father caught sight of him, and was filled with compassion. He ran to his son, embraced him and kissed him. His son said to him, 'Father, I have sinned against heaven and against you; I no longer deserve to be called your son.' But his father ordered his servants, 'Quickly, bring the finest robe and put it on him; put a ring on his finger and sandals on his feet. Take the fattened calf and slaughter it. Then let us celebrate with a feast, because this son of mine was dead, and has come to life again; he was lost, and has been found.' Then the celebration began. Now the older son had been out in the field and, on his way back, as he neared the house, he heard the sound of music and dancing. He called one of the servants and asked what this might mean. The servant said to him, 'Your brother has returned and your father has slaughtered the fattened calf because he has him back safe and sound.' He became angry, and when he refused to enter the house, his father came out and pleaded with him. He said to his father in reply, 'Look, all these years I served you and not once did I disobey your orders; yet you never gave me even a young goat to feast on with my friends. But when your son returns who swallowed up your property with prostitutes, for him you slaughter the fattened calf.' He said to him, 'My son, you are here with me always; everything I have is yours. But now we must celebrate and rejoice, because your brother was dead and has come to life again; he was lost and has been found.'"

LUKE 15: 1-3, 11-32

SAINT BENEDICT

"The abbot must indeed exercise very great care, and hasten with all keeness and energy to prevent any of the sheep in his care from being lost."

RB 27.5

REFLECTION

One of the most well-beloved of the parables of Jesus is the parable of the Prodigal Son. It is the third in a series of parables which deal with the lost being found, beginning with the lost sheep, then the lost coin, and finally the lost son. In each instance when what was lost is found, there is cause of great rejoicing and celebration. Saint Benedict understood that the monks of the monastery would often find themselves succumbing to temptation, but he did not want the abbot to give up on those monks, but to be for them like the Good Shepherd, like the good father who seeks to restore the lost to the joy of the life of grace.

How often do we rejoice that the Lord has called each of us by name and given us a share in his kingdom? How often do we thank God for receiving us back when we have sinned and for offering us the Sacraments of Reconciliation and the Holy Eucharist so that we might be strengthened and refreshed for the difficulties and trials of our daily crosses? On this Laetáre Sunday, let us rejoice in the power of God's goodness and be one with him in seeking out what was lost and rejoicing when it finds its way home.

PRAYER

Lord Jesus, you never abandon us, even in our sinfulness, but call to us daily to turn away from evil and come back to you. As we journey through Lent, help us to be steadfast in the gifts you have given us and seek you with all our hearts. You live and reign forever and ever. Amen.

GOSPEL

At that time Jesus left [Samaria] for Galilee. For Jesus himself testified that a prophet has no honor in his native place. When he came into Galilee, the Galileans welcomed him, since they had seen all he had done in Jerusalem at the feast; for they themselves had gone to the feast.

Then he returned to Cana in Galilee, where he had made the water wine. Now there was a royal official whose son was ill in Capernaum. When he heard that Jesus had arrived in Galilee from Judea, he went to him and asked him to come down and heal his son, who was near death. Jesus said to him, "Unless you people see signs and wonders, you will not believe." The royal official said to him, "Sir, come down before my child dies." Jesus said to him, "You may go; your son will live." The man believed what Jesus said to him and left. While the man was on his way back, his slaves met him and told him that his boy would live. He asked them when he began to recover. They told him, "The fever left him yesterday, about one in the afternoon." The father realized that just at that time Jesus had said to him, "Your son will live," and he and his whole household came to believe. Now this was the second sign Jesus did when he came to Galilee from Judea.

JOHN 4: 43-54

SAINT BENEDICT

"Prayer should be short and pure."

RB 20.4a

REFLECTION

During these final three weeks of Lent, its "second semester," as it were, the focus of the Gospels shifts from teachings of Jesus that demand and encourage genuine conversion of the heart and the practice of the disciplines of Lent (prayer, fasting, and almsgiving) to the mystery of Christ's passion and death. Now we will read of Jesus' confronting and defying the growing opposition and death plots which his detractors and enemies hatched against him. Yet even in the midst of the clamor of this aggression and hostility toward him and his message, Jesus is able to hear and respond with great generosity and love to those who put their trust in him. The royal official's simple and poignant plea, repeated twice, "Come down and heal my son," moves the Lord to speak but a word and not only restore life to the son but also restore the spirit and heart of the father and the whole family to praise God.

Saint Benedict taught his monks that their prayer ought to be "short and pure," for the Lord has no need for long and elaborate formulas. In the words of the prophet Micah: "You have been told, O man, what is good, and what the Lord requires of you: Only to do right and to love goodness, and to walk humbly with your God."

PRAYER

Heavenly Father, hear the prayer we offer you today. With the childlike simplicity your Son asked of his followers, we beg you to grant us the grace to hear your word and act according to it every day of our lives. We make this prayer through Christ our Lord. Amen.

GOSPEL

There was a feast of the Jews, and Jesus went up to Jerusalem. Now there is in Jerusalem at the Sheep Gate a pool called in Hebrew Bethesda, with five porticoes. In these lay a large number of ill, blind, lame, and crippled. One man was there who had been ill for thirty-eight years. When Jesus saw him lying there and knew that he had been ill for a long time, he said to him, "Do you want to be well?" The sick man answered him, "Sir, I have no one to put me into the pool when the water is stirred up; while I am on my way, someone else gets down there before me." Jesus said to him, "Rise, take up your mat, and walk." Immediately the man became well, took up his mat, and walked.

Now that day was a sabbath. So the Jews said to the man who was cured, "It is the sabbath, and it is not lawful for you to carry your mat." He answered them, "The man who made me well told me, 'Take up your mat and walk.'" They asked him, "Who is the man who told you, 'Take it up and walk'?" The man who was healed did not know who it was, for Jesus had slipped away, since there was a crowd there. After this Jesus found him in the temple area and said to him, "Look, you are well; do not sin any more, so that nothing worse may happen to you." The man went and told the Jews that Jesus was the one who had made him well. Therefore, the Jews began to persecute Jesus because he did this on a sabbath.

JOHN 5: 1-16

SAINT BENEDICT

"What could be sweeter, dearest brothers, than this voice of the Lord, who invites us? Look, the Lord in his devotion to us shows us the way to life."

RB PROLOGUE 19–20

REFLECTION

In many of the situations in which Jesus performed a healing miracle, the sick person, or someone on his or her behalf, approached Jesus and asked for assistance. The sick man in today's Gospel suffered for thirty-eight years. He nonetheless waited patiently by the pool called Bethesda for the waters to be stirred and for someone then to help him into the pool. When Jesus first came up to him, perhaps he thought Jesus would assist him to the pool. He was not looking for a miracle, not expecting a miracle. He just wanted a bit of help. But of all the blind, lame, and sick by the pool, Jesus goes to this man and, to the man's great wonder and surprise, with a single word completely healed him.

God calls to each of us by name and wishes to speak to our hearts, for his love for each of us is without end. Yet we so often are not even looking for that presence in our lives. A bit of help here and there, perhaps, but certainly we are not looking for or expecting the power of God to be made manifest to us. But it is there, waiting to reveal itself to us when our hearts and minds are open to the wonder of God's love. It is there, to enable us to stand firm in faith, to be joyful in hope, and to love one another as God has loved us.

PRAYER

Heavenly Father, grant us your healing grace that we might sing the wonders of your love in an endless chorus of praise with Saint Benedict, and all the saints and angels. We ask this through Christ our Lord. Amen.

GOSPEL

Jesus answered the Jews: "My Father is at work until now, so I am at work." For this reason they tried all the more to kill him, because he not only broke the sabbath but he also called God his own father, making himself equal to God.

Jesus answered and said to them, "Amen, amen, I say to you, the Son cannot do anything on his own, but only what he sees the Father doing; for what he does, the Son will do also. For the Father loves the Son and shows him everything that he himself does, and he will show him greater works than these, so that you may be amazed. For just as the Father raises the dead and gives life, so also does the Son give life to whomever he wishes. Nor does the Father judge anyone, but he has given all judgment to the Son, so that all may honor the Son just as they honor the Father. Whoever does not honor the Son does not honor the Father who sent him. Amen, amen, I say to you, whoever hears my word and believes in the one who sent me has eternal life and will not come to condemnation, but has passed from death to life. Amen, amen, I say to you, the hour is coming and is now here when the dead will hear the voice of the Son of God, and those who hear will live. For just as the Father has life in himself, so also he gave to the Son the possession of life in himself. And he gave him power to exercise judgment, because he is the Son of Man. Do not be amazed at this, because the hour is coming in which all who are in the tombs will hear his voice and will come out, those who have done good deeds to the resurrection of life, but those who have done wicked deeds to the resurrection of condemnation.

"I cannot do anything on my own; I judge as I hear, and my judgment is just, because I do not seek my own will but the will of the one who sent me."

JOHN 5: 17-30

SAINT BENEDICT

"It is love that drives these people to progress toward eternal life. Therefore they seize on the narrow way."

RB 5.10–11

REFLECTION

"They tried all the more to kill him." The contrast between the work that Jesus came to do and the work of his enemies is brought into sharp focus in this Gospel passage from Saint John. While the enemies of Jesus sought his death, Jesus over and over again spoke and acted for life. Indeed the words "life" and "live" are spoken by Jesus some eight times in these fourteen verses. The work of Jesus was to give eternal life: he did the Father's will by offering life; he honored the Father by preaching and teaching about life and performing miraculous signs of life; he invited all who heard him to be rejuvenated and made joyful in life; he forgave and loved his enemies, as he taught his disciples to do. His work was to bring to its full meaning the words of the prophet Isaiah: "For the Lord comforts his people and shows mercy to his afflicted. . . . Can a mother forget her infant, be without tenderness for the child of her womb? Even should she forget, I will never forget you" (Is 49:15).

Do we have a love and a yearning for eternal life? Although Saint Benedict was well aware of the difficulties and hardships around him, he understood that only in the context of eternal life can this life have any meaning. Our Lenten discipline, our own little "narrow way," is a time for us to re-center our lives on a loving God who is ever calling us to eternal life.

PRAYER

Lord God, source of all life, you sent your son as the Resurrection and the Life in fulfillment of your covenantal promise to be God-with-us. May we strive after this gift of eternal life and, by your grace, may we help to win over others to this promised life by the merits of your son, Jesus Christ, who is Lord forever and ever. Amen.

GOSPEL

JESUS SAID TO THE JEWS:

"If I testify on my own behalf, my testimony is not true. But there is another who testifies on my behalf, and I know that the testimony he gives on my behalf is true. You sent emissaries to John, and he testified to the truth. I do not accept human testimony, but I say this so that you may be saved. He was a burning and shining lamp, and for a while you were content to rejoice in his light. But I have testimony greater than John's. The works that the Father gave me to accomplish, these works that I perform testify on my behalf that the Father has sent me. Moreover, the Father who sent me has testified on my behalf. But you have never heard his voice nor seen his form, and you do not have his word remaining in you, because you do not believe in the one whom he has sent. You search the Scriptures, because you think you have eternal life through them; even they testify on my behalf. But you do not want to come to me to have life.

"I do not accept human praise; moreover, I know that you do not have the love of God in you. I came in the name of my Father, but you do not accept me; yet if another comes in his own name, you will accept him. How can you believe, when you accept praise from one another and do not seek the praise that comes from the only God? Do not think that I will accuse you before the Father: the one who will accuse you is Moses, in whom you have placed your hope. For if you had believed Moses, you would have believed me, because he wrote about me. But if you do not believe his writings, how will you believe my words?"

JOHN 5: 31-47

SAINT BENEDICT

"The Lord, seeking a worker for himself in the crowds to whom he cries out, says: 'Which of you desires life and longs to see good days?' (Ps 34:13)."

RB PROLOGUE 14–15

REFLECTION

The murderous hostility on the part of some who were deeply offended by Jesus' healing on the Sabbath of the sick man at the pool of Bethesda elicited from Jesus the response recounted in today's Gospel. Yet as he talked about the testimony that gives witness to his person as sent by God, especially according to the very Scriptures which his enemies were trying to use against him, there is the sense that all the while he spoke he was searching the crowd for those who would be moved to consider again the words of the Scripture and come to the realization that what Jesus was saying was indeed true. Some there, Jesus knew, who had the love of God in their hearts and who therefore could begin to hear and understand Jesus' words that revealed God's plan for the redemption of humankind. Even in the midst of growing antagonism and death threats, Jesus continued to seek out those who in turn were truly seeking God and who would listen in their hearts to the voice of the Lord calling to them.

Saint Benedict knew that unless the love of God was in our hearts, we would not be able to hear his voice. Thus he called on all his monks, whatever their time in or experience of monastic life, never to stop their search for God, never to draw back from the quest to become more and more conformed to the will of the Father revealed in the Son.

PRAYER

Lord God, may our hearts rejoice as we search for you, confident that you are always present to us even in the midst of trial and sorrow, and that you draw us closer to you when, by your grace, we seek you in our daily lives. Hear us, gracious God, and bless our efforts in this season of Lent to turn to you. We make this prayer through Christ our Lord. Amen.

GOSPEL

Jesus moved about within Galilee; he did not wish to travel in Judea, because the Jews were trying to kill him. But the Jewish feast of Tabernacles was near.

But when his brothers had gone up to the feast, he himself also went up, not openly but as it were in secret.

Some of the inhabitants of Jerusalem said, "Is he not the one they are trying to kill? And look, he is speaking openly and they say nothing to him. Could the authorities have realized that he is the Christ? But we know where he is from. When the Christ comes, no one will know where he is from." So Jesus cried out in the temple area as he was teaching and said, "You know me and also know where I am from. Yet I did not come on my own, but the one who sent me, whom you do not know, is true. I know him, because I am from him, and he sent me." So they tried to arrest him, but no one laid a hand upon him, because his hour had not yet come.

JOHN 7: 1-2, 10, 25-30

SAINT BENEDICT

"Fear Judgment Day. Have a healthy fear of hell."

RB 4.44–45

REFLECTION

Saint Benedict is not reticent or shy about the seriousness of sin. Like all the holy women and men of God, he is horrified by sin for it was because of sin that the Father sent his Son to take upon himself all the consequences of the sins of the world: "Love, then, consists in this: not that we have loved God, but that he has loved us and has sent his Son as an offering for our sins" (1 Jn 4:10). The suffering he was to endure for our salvation was not just the physical agony of the Garden of Gethsemani and the Praetorium and Calvary, but also the moral and emotional suffering of the plotting, betrayal, desertion, and rejection by the very people whom he had come to save. So sin is not some trifle in Saint Benedict's mind: it is that which added to Christ's suffering and it is that for which we bear responsibility. Benedict's admonitions in chapter 4, that issue warnings about judgment and eternal damnation, then, are not simply scare tactics to elicit good behavior; they are serious calls to a mature faith in order that we might fight sin with all the powers given by God and that we might further strive to share in the sufferings of Christ.

The disciplines of Lent can be seen to have this same twofold purpose, made most poignant when on Ash Wednesday our foreheads are signed with the sign of the cross in ashes and we are bidden: "Turn away from sin and be faithful to the gospel."

PRAYER

Lord, you are close to the brokenhearted because you experienced all aspects of our condition, except for sin. Hear the prayers of your people: help us to turn from sin and to be ever more faithful to our baptismal promises. You live and reign forever and ever. Amen.

GOSPEL

Some in the crowd who heard these words of Jesus said, "This is truly the Prophet." Others said, "This is the Christ." But others said, "The Christ will not come from Galilee, will he? Does not Scripture say that the Christ will be of David's family and come from Bethlehem, the village where David lived?" So a division occurred in the crowd because of him. Some of them even wanted to arrest him, but no one laid hands on him.

So the guards went to the chief priests and Pharisees, who asked them, "Why did you not bring him?" The guards answered, "Never before has anyone spoken like this man." So the Pharisees answered them, "Have you also been deceived? Have any of the authorities or the Pharisees believed in him? But this crowd, which does not know the law, is accursed." Nicodemus, one of their members who had come to him earlier, said to them, "Does our law condemn a man before it first hears him and finds out what he is doing?" They answered and said to him, "You are not from Galilee also, are you? Look and see that no prophet arises from Galilee."

Then each went to his own house.

JOHN 7: 40-53

SAINT BENEDICT

"The workshop where we should work hard at all these things is the monastic enclosure and stability in the community."

RB 4.78

REFLECTION

The enclosure of the monastery, the cloister, is not for Saint Benedict a means of entrapping or restricting the movement of the monks. Rather it is meant first to express their complete devotion to the seeking of God by following a monastic manner of life and fulfilling their vows of obedience, stability, and conversion. Second, it is a means of securing to as great an extent as possible their ability to order their lives according to the teachings of the Gospel and the Rule that they can create the atmosphere as well as to have the time to adhere as closely as possible to the admonition of Saint Paul "to pray always." Third, it is a sign of their solidarity, of their like-mindedness as a community of believing Christians who profess Jesus as Lord in all they say and do.

The Gospel passage for today reveals the dissension and division of those who refused to recognize Jesus as Lord, and it concludes with the ominous judgment: "Then each went to his own house" (Jn 7:53). Lent is a time for all Christians to be reunited in their faith, hope, and love in the service of the one true God.

PRAYER

Lord God, we have sinned against you and against your love, and so have sown the seeds of discord and disunity in our world. During this season of Lent may we come to be more fully united to your Church and your people, so that we might raise our voices as one to the glory of your name. We ask this through Christ our Lord. Amen.

FIFTH WEEK
OF
LENT

GOSPEL

Now a man was ill, Lazarus from Bethany, the village of Mary and her sister Martha. Mary was the one who had anointed the Lord with perfumed oil and dried his feet with her hair; it was her brother Lazarus who was ill. So the sisters sent word to Jesus saying, "Master, the one you love is ill." When Jesus heard this he said, "This illness is not to end in death, but is for the glory of God, that the Son of God may be glorified through it." Now Jesus loved Martha and her sister and Lazarus. So when he heard that he was ill, he remained for two days in the place where he was. Then after this he said to his disciples, "Let us go back to Judea." The disciples said to him, "Rabbi, the Jews were just trying to stone you, and you want to go back there?" Jesus answered, "Are there not twelve hours in a day? If one walks during the day, he does not stumble, because he sees the light of this world. But if one walks at night, he stumbles, because the light is not in him." He said this, and then told them, "Our friend Lazarus is asleep, but I am going to awaken him." So the disciples said to him, "Master, if he is asleep, he will be saved." But Jesus was talking about his death, while they thought that he meant ordinary sleep. So then Jesus said to them clearly, "Lazarus has died. And I am glad for you that I was not there, that you may believe. Let us go to him." So Thomas, called Didymus, said to his fellow disciples, "Let us also go to die with him."

When Jesus arrived, he found that Lazarus had already been in the tomb for four days. Now Bethany was near Jerusalem, only about two miles away. And many of the Jews had come to Martha and Mary to comfort them about their brother. When Martha heard that Jesus was coming, she went to meet him; but Mary sat at home. Martha said to Jesus, "Lord, if you had been here, my brother would not have died. But even now I know that whatever you ask of God, God will give you."

Jesus said to her, "Your brother will rise." Martha said to him, "I know he will rise, in the resurrection on the last day." Jesus told her, "I am the resurrection and the life; whoever believes in me, even if he dies, will live, and everyone who lives and believes in me will never die. Do you believe this?" She said to him, "Yes, Lord. I have come to believe that you are the Christ, the Son of God, the one who is coming into the world."

When she had said this, she went and called her sister Mary secretly, saying, "The teacher is here and is asking for you." As soon as she heard this, she rose quickly and went to him. For Jesus had not yet come into the village, but was still where Martha had met him. So when the Jews who were with her in the house comforting her saw Mary get up quickly and go out, they followed her, presuming that she was going to the tomb to weep there. When Mary came to where Jesus was and saw him, she fell at his feet and said to him, "Lord, if you had been here, my brother would not have died." When Jesus saw her weeping and the Jews who had come with her weeping, he became perturbed and deeply troubled, and said, "Where have you laid him?" They said to him, "Sir, come and see." And Jesus wept. So the Jews said, "See how he loved him." But some of them said, "Could not the one who opened the eyes of the blind man have done something so that this man would not have died?"

So Jesus, perturbed again, came to the tomb. It was a cave, and a stone lay across it. Jesus said, "Take away the stone." Martha, the dead man's sister, said to him, "Lord, by now there will be a stench; he has been dead for four days." Jesus said to her, "Did I not tell you that if you believe you will see the glory of God?" So they took away the stone. And Jesus raised his eyes and said, "Father, I thank you for hearing me. I know that you always hear me; but because of the crowd here I have said this, that they may believe that you sent me." And when he had said this, he cried out in a loud voice, "Lazarus, come out!" The dead man came out, tied hand and foot with burial bands, and his face was wrapped in a cloth. So Jesus said to them, "Untie him and let him go."

Now many of the Jews who had come to Mary and seen what he had done began to believe in him.

JOHN 11: 1-45

Shorter form: JOHN 11:3-7, 17, 20-27, 33b-45
Longer form may be optionally read on any day in the fifth week of Lent

SAINT BENEDICT

"Put your hope in God."

RB 4.41

REFLECTION

In addition to the Rule of Saint Benedict, each monastery today has what is commonly called a "Book of Customs," a document that describes how that particular monastery lives out in its day-to-day life the vision of Saint Benedict. In my community's Book of Customs, the following passage begins the section on the death of a confrere: "The bond of the common life is too strong and too full of faith to be confined to this life only. When one of the monks of the community is called to eternal life and the vision of God, the community does not mourn without hope. Rather, the consolations of faith allow the community to offer thanks to God for his gifts and to offer supplications for the departed confrere that God be merciful to him. For when one of the confreres, having persevered in the monastery until death, is called home to God, the community's hope of one day being reunited in Christ strengthens the bonds of mutual love and concern, and the pilgrim Church becomes more closely united with the heavenly Church."

Jesus placed his hope in God and he invited others to discover the riches and beauty of God's love for them in their lives by living in a hope grounded in God alone. As Lent moves ever closer to Holy Week and the Paschal Triduum and Easter, and as the season of spring brings light and warmth and color, so may hope in God fill our hearts.

PRAYER

You, O God, are our refuge in time of trouble and difficulty and with you alone is mercy and fullness of redemption. Hear the prayers of your people who look to you and grant that we may be faithful in doing your will every day of our lives. We make this prayer through Christ our Lord. Amen.

GOSPEL

Some Greeks who had come to worship at the Passover Feast came to Philip, who was from Bethsaida in Galilee, and asked him, "Sir, we would like to see Jesus." Philip went and told Andrew; then Andrew and Philip went and told Jesus. Jesus answered them, "The hour has come for the Son of Man to be glorified. Amen, amen, I say to you, unless a grain of wheat falls to the ground and dies, it remains just a grain of wheat; but if it dies, it produces much fruit. Whoever loves his life loses it, and whoever hates his life in this world will preserve it for eternal life. Whoever serves me must follow me, and where I am, there also will my servant be. The Father will honor whoever serves me.

"I am troubled now. Yet what should I say? 'Father, save me from this hour'? But it was for this purpose that I came to this hour. Father, glorify your name." Then a voice came from heaven, "I have glorified it and will glorify it again." The crowd there heard it and said it was thunder; but others said, "An angel has spoken to him." Jesus answered and said, "This voice did not come for my sake but for yours. Now is the time of judgement on this world; now the ruler of this world will be driven out. And when I am lifted up from the earth, I will draw everyone to myself." He said this indicating the kind of death he would die.

JOHN 12: 20-33

SAINT BENEDICT

"On account of the holy service they have professed, and because of a fear of hell and the glory of eternal life, as soon as something is commanded by the superior, they waste no time in executing it as if it were divinely commanded."

RB 5.3–4

REFLECTION

In the Rule of Saint Benedict, obedience is always understood as an eager listening for and a prompt response to the Word of God as it is made manifest to the monks, first, in the orders of the abbot, who "is believe to represent Christ in the monastery" (RB 2.2), and, second, in the needs of all the members of the community, both young and old, for "the blessing of obedience is not only something that everyone ought to show the abbot, but the brothers should also obey one another" (RB 71.1). It is in the way that they choose to follow the narrow way that leads to heaven and the glory of everlasting life with the Blessed Virgin Mary and all the saints and angels. Saint Benedict wanted in one mystery of faith to bring together obedience and service and glory. But Saint Benedict is no idealist; he was not trying to create a utopian society but to provide a way of living that recognized the reality of sin as well as the reality of the redemptive and freely offered grace of God. He understood that living such a life faithfully day by day required sacrifice and surrender of one's own will, in imitation of Christ, for he knew that "unless the grain of wheat falls to the earth and dies, it remains just a grain of wheat. But if it dies, it produces much fruit" (Jn 12:24).

In Lent we all have an opportunity to learn the lesson of the grain of wheat and to renew our commitment to listen for and respond generously to the Word of God.

PRAYER

God of power and might, you call us to share in the glory of your only Son by dying to self and rising to new life in him. May your Church serve you as it serves those who lack the necessities of life, those who are unable to defend themselves, and those who live in hopelessness that they may come to know and love you as their one true God. We make this prayer through Christ our Lord. Amen.

GOSPEL

Jesus went to the Mount of Olives. But early in the morning he arrived again in the temple area, and all the people started coming to him, and he sat down and taught them. Then the scribes and the Pharisees brought a woman who had been caught in adultery and made her stand in the middle. They said to him, "Teacher, this woman was caught in the very act of committing adultery. Now in the law, Moses commanded us to stone such women. So what do you say?" They said this to test him, so that they could have some charge to bring against him. Jesus bent down and began to write on the ground with his finger. But when they continued asking him, he straightened up and said to them, "Let the one among you who is without sin be the first to throw a stone at her." Again he bent down and wrote on the ground. And in response, they went away one by one, beginning with the elders. So he was left alone with the woman before him. Then Jesus straightened up and said to her, "Woman, where are they? Has no one condemned you?" She replied, "No one, sir." Then Jesus said, "Neither do I condemn you. Go, and from now on do not sin any more."

JOHN 8: 1-11

SAINT BENEDICT

"The seventh step of humility is surmounted if the monk not only confesses with his tongue, but also believes with all his heart that he is lower and less honorable than all the rest."

RB 7.51

REFLECTION

The scribes and Pharisees who brought the woman caught in adultery to Jesus were not humble men. They did not see into the evil that lurked in their own hearts but were quick to judge and condemn others. They never understood the truth that any person's sin was a sin that they themselves could commit. In the tradition of the Desert Christians of the early centuries, a tradition with which Saint Benedict was familiar, this is a common theme. Here, for example, is a story about the fourth century hermit Abba Bessarion: "A brother who had sinned was turned out of the church by the priest; Abba Bessarion got up and went with him, saying, 'I, too, am a sinner.'"[1] The person who is humble like that, humble as Saint Benedict taught his monks to be by the seventh step of humility, is truly walking in the way of Christ.

The Sacrament of Reconciliation is a graced moment for those who readily and humbly acknowledge their sinfulness and seek the forgiveness and the loving embrace of the Lord. As the great days of Holy Week draw near, now is a good time to avail ourselves of this joyful sacrament that we might be renewed to worship the Lord in Spirit and in truth.

PRAYER

Lord God, you have done great things for us and made us glad. May we rejoice in your gift of forgiveness and learn to offer that same forgiveness in peace and in sincerity of heart to all who may have offended us. We ask this in the name of Jesus your Son. Amen.

---

1 *The Desert Christian: The Sayings of the Desert Fathers,* trans. Benedicta Ward (New York: Macmillan, 1975), 42.

GOSPEL

Jesus went to the Mount of Olives. But early in the morning he arrived again in the temple area, and all the people started coming to him, and he sat down and taught them. Then the scribes and the Pharisees brought a woman who had been caught in adultery and made her stand in the middle. They said to him, "Teacher, this woman was caught in the very act of committing adultery. Now in the law, Moses commanded us to stone such women. So what do you say?" They said this to test him, so that they could have some charge to bring against him. Jesus bent down and began to write on the ground with his finger. But when they continued asking him, he straightened up and said to them, "Let the one among you who is without sin be the first to throw a stone at her." Again he bent down and wrote on the ground. And in response, they went away one by one, beginning with the elders. So he was left alone with the woman before him. Then Jesus straightened up and said to her, "Woman, where are they? Has no one condemned you?" She replied, "No one, sir." Then Jesus said, "Neither do I condemn you. Go, and from now on do not sin any more."

JOHN 8: 1-11

SAINT BENEDICT

"Do not give a false peace."

RB 4.25

REFLECTION

The Pharisees addressed Jesus by the formal and respectful title "Teacher." Yet their intentions were anything but respectful. It is indeed most insincere, for their purpose was to trap and condemn Jesus, whom they knew to have a great sympathy for and a disposition of forgiveness toward even the worst sinners, despite the dictates of the Law of Moses. A retreat master once told us that in the ancient world those who crafted images of the gods and goddesses for sale in the marketplace would cover up the imperfections in the bronze figurines with wax and paint. If a customer wanted a statue without imperfections, one that was genuine, he would ask for one without wax, in Latin *sine cere*, from which our word "sincere" derives. The Pharisees lack sincerity.

While Saint Benedict's admonition never to offer a false or insincere peace appears simple, it is in fact asking quite a lot. It is asking the monks to be truly genuine and sincere in their relations with one another, with their superiors, with the guests and the poor, and indeed with the Lord. Lent is a good time to examine our sincerity and to resolve never again to be hollow or insincere or false in our relations with others.

PRAYER

Lord Jesus, you forgave the woman taken in adultery whom others had condemned. When our consciences are burdened with sin, let us never lose hope in your mercy and so lead lives that are upright and sincere. You live and reign for ever and ever. Amen.

In Year C, when the preceding Gospel is read on Sunday, the following text is used.

GOSPEL

Jesus spoke to them again, saying, "I am the light of the world. Whoever follows me will not walk in darkness, but will have the light of life." So the Pharisees said to him, "You testify on your own behalf, so your testimony cannot be verified." Jesus answered and said to them, "Even if I do testify on my own behalf, my testimony can be verified, because I know where I came from and where I am going. But you do not know where I come from or where I am going. You judge by appearances, but I do not judge anyone. And even if I should judge, my judgment is valid, because I am not alone, but it is I and the Father who sent me. Even in your law it is written that the testimony of two men can be verified. I testify on my behalf and so does the Father who sent me." So they said to him, "Where is your father?" Jesus answered, "You know neither me nor my Father. If you knew me, you would know my Father also." He spoke these words while teaching in the treasury in the temple area. But no one arrested him, because his hour had not yet come.

JOHN 8: 12-20

SAINT BENEDICT

"Vigils should be followed by Matins at daybreak."

RB 8.4

REFLECTION

The monks of Saint Benedict's monastery gathered together eight times a day for common prayer, which in the monastic tradition is called the Opus Dei, the Work of God. Saint Benedict specified the times during the day for these hours of prayer. Vigils, for example, took place very early in the morning, well before the rising of the sun. Vigils is a reminder of the expectant waiting, the "waiting in joyful hope" for the coming of the Lord, as the prayer recited by the priest after the Lord's Prayer at Mass has it, just as the bridesmaids with burning torches were to wait through the night to welcome the bridegroom (Mt 25:1–13). Matins, the great morning prayer of praise, is to take place at dawn with the first arrival of the sun rising in the east (in Latin, *incipiente luce*). The sun, the daystar in the east, is for the monks a great sign of the Son of God, the light of the world. For "he, the Dayspring, shall visit us in his mercy to shine on those who sit in darkness and the shadow of death, to guide our feet into the way of peace" (Lk 1:78–79).

The lengthening of daylight as Lent progresses toward Easter provides us with an image of the light of Christ that can continue to grow within us if we choose with his grace to live in imitation of him all our days.

PRAYER

Heavenly Father, you sent your Son as light of the world to guide us to heaven so that there we might sing your praises with all the choirs of saints and angels. May we receive the Light of Christ at Easter in thanksgiving and joy, and help to spread his light to all the world. We ask this through Christ our Lord. Amen.

GOSPEL

JESUS SAID TO THE PHARISEES:

"I am going away and you will look for me, but you will die in your sin. Where I am going you cannot come." So the Jews said, "He is not going to kill himself, is he, because he said, 'Where I am going you cannot come'?" He said to them, "You belong to what is below, I belong to what is above. You belong to this world, but I do not belong to this world. That is why I told you that you will die in your sins. For if you do not believe that I AM, you will die in your sins." So they said to him, "Who are you?" Jesus said to them, "What I told you from the beginning. I have much to say about you in condemnation. But the one who sent me is true, and what I heard from him I tell the world." They did not realize that he was speaking to them of the Father. So Jesus said to them, "When you lift up the Son of Man, then you will realize that I AM, and that I do nothing on my own, but I say only what the Father taught me. The one who sent me is with me. He has not left me alone, because I always do what is pleasing to him." Because he spoke this way, many came to believe in him.

JOHN 8: 21-30

SAINT BENEDICT

"The towering ladder [of humility] is, of course, our earthly life. When the heart is humble, God raises it up to heaven. We could say that our body and soul are the sides of this ladder, into which the divine summons has inserted various rungs of humility and discipline for the ascent."

RB 7.8–9

REFLECTION

Jesus distinguished himself from the Pharisees by claiming to be "from above" while they were "from below." It was because of this opposition that the Pharisees were simply unable to understand either Jesus or his mission. We experience this "from above" and "from below" in our own lives and in our own persons. We experience at times the movement of grace that comes "from above" and that invites us and moves us to imitate Christ in his loving kindness and tender mercy. Yet we also experience the power of temptation and sin that comes "from below" and that draws us down from the life we are called to lead by the Lord. The cross of Christ must be for us the fixed point in our spiritual lives according to which we can determine what is "from above" and what is "from below."

Saint Benedict understood this idea of "from above" and "from below" and used the analogy of a ladder, based on the ladder about which Jacob dreamed (Gen 28:12), to teach his monks to avoid the beckoning allure that comes "from below" and to take rather the steps of humility and discipline by which one can ascend to the perfect love of God which casts our fear (RB 7.67). Lent affords us an opportunity to turn away from what is below in us and to strive in grace for what is above.

PRAYER

Instruct us in your way, O Lord, and teach us to follow with gladness the narrow path that leads to life eternal. May we embrace humility and the discipline of this Lent and so come to the joys of heaven, where you live and reign forever and ever. Amen.

GOSPEL

Jesus said to those Jews who believed in him, "If you remain in my word, you will truly be my disciples, and you will know the truth, and the truth will set you free." They answered him, "We are descendants of Abraham and have never been enslaved to anyone. How can you say, 'You will become free'?" Jesus answered them, "Amen, amen, I say to you, everyone who commits sin is a slave of sin. A slave does not remain in a household forever, but a son always remains. So if the Son frees you, then you will truly be free. I know that you are descendants of Abraham. But you are trying to kill me, because my word has no room among you. I tell you what I have seen in the Father's presence; then do what you have heard from the Father."

They answered and said to him, "Our father is Abraham." Jesus said to them, "If you were Abraham's children, you would be doing the works of Abraham. But now you are trying to kill me, a man who has told you the truth that I heard from God; Abraham did not do this. You are doing the works of your father!" So they said to him, "We were not born of fornication. We have one Father, God." Jesus said to them, "If God were your Father, you would love me, for I came from God and am here; I did not come on my own, but he sent me."

JOHN 8: 31-42

SAINT BENEDICT

"Thus you will return by the labor of obedience to the one from whom you drifted through the inertia of disobedience."

RB PROLOGUE 2

REFLECTION

For Saint Benedict, obedience is a labor, a work. It is often hard and arduous. But it is the only way to the Lord. For it is only in the labor of obedience that the monk can come to an understanding of and to live out in his day-to-day life the truth of Christ's own obedience, which was unto death on a cross (RB 7.34). In Christ's obedience, the monk can discover that to abide in the truth which Christ revealed is the only way to be free from the power of sin and to be free to love God and neighbor with devotion and fervor. A willing listening for and obedience to this truth is the only way, though it is a narrow way, to the freedom promised to the children of God. Any other way may appear to be free, but it is truly enslavement to the whims of one's own desires and passions. Saint Benedict calls this "inertia" out of which one cannot break into freedom unless one is obedient to the teachings of Christ. The duty and the obligation of freedom are to live in accord with the truth. It is only the truth that is Christ, who is the Way, the Truth, and the Light, which alone can set us free.

The disciplines of Lent, freely embraced, can help us to be obedient to the truth that Christ revealed. By our obedience to this truth we are not only truly free to love but we are also brought closer and closer to unity with the Father.

PRAYER

Instruct us, O Lord, in your way and on an even path lead us that filled with the spirit of charity and humility we may serve the needs of our sisters and brothers and so by joyful obedience be united with you, who with the Father and the Holy Spirit live and reign forever and ever. Amen.

GOSPEL

JESUS SAID TO THE JEWS:

"Amen, amen, I say to you, whoever keeps my word will never see death." So the Jews said to him, "Now we are sure that you are possessed. Abraham died, as did the prophets, yet you say, 'Whoever keeps my word will never taste death.' Are you greater than our father Abraham, who died? Or the prophets, who died? Who do you make yourself out to be?" Jesus answered, "If I glorify myself, my glory is worth nothing; but it is my Father who glorifies me, of whom you say, 'He is our God.' You do not know him, but I know him. And if I should say that I do not know him, I would be like you a liar. But I do know him and I keep his word. Abraham your father rejoiced to see my day; he saw it and was glad." So the Jews said to him, "You are not yet fifty years old and you have seen Abraham?" Jesus said to them, "Amen, amen, I say to you, before Abraham came to be, I AM." So they picked up stones to throw at him; but Jesus hid and went out of the temple area.

JOHN 8: 51-59

SAINT BENEDICT

"And if we wish to flee the punishment of hell and attain eternal life, while there is still time and we are still in this body, and there remains time to accomplish all this in the light of this life, we must run and accomplish now what will profit us for eternity."

RB PROLOGUE 42–44

REFLECTION

Many times in his Rule, Saint Benedict urged his monks to run, to hurry, to hasten along the way that leads to life. Today perhaps we might call this a spiritual "carpe diem," a seizing of the day. To stand still appeared to Saint Benedict to be the same as moving backwards. Each moment is an opportunity for grace to work in us, for hearing the voice of God speaking to us in a variety of persons, for obeying that voice in our devotion to our families, friends, co-workers, and indeed to all people, for making our work and occupations freewill offerings to God, for making prayer a regular component of our daily lives.

Those who confronted Jesus in today's Gospel were not seizing the day. They were living in the past and had closed themselves to any possibility of any understanding or grasp of the past in terms of the new revelation that Jesus wished to teach them. They had thus closed themselves to realizing the fullness of meaning of the prophecies and images of the Scriptures of the Old Law. On this day of Lent, while there remains time for us, let us be open to the manifold presence of God in our lives and "accomplish now what will profit us for eternity."

PRAYER

Heavenly Father, your grace is abundant and generous, and you shower your blessings on us each day. Help us to use our allotted time to draw closer to you and to live in peace with all people. We make this prayer through Christ our Lord. Amen.

GOSPEL

The Jews picked up rocks to stone Jesus. Jesus answered them, "I have shown you many good works from my Father. For which of these are you trying to stone me?" The Jews answered him, "We are not stoning you for a good work but for blasphemy. You, a man, are making yourself God." Jesus answered them, "Is it not written in your law, 'I said, "You are gods"'? If it calls them gods to whom the word of God came, and Scripture cannot be set aside, can you say that the one whom the Father has consecrated and sent into the world blasphemes because I said, 'I am the Son of God'? If I do not perform my Father's works, do not believe me; but if I perform them, even if you do not believe me, believe the works, so that you may realize and understand that the Father is in me and I am in the Father." Then they tried again to arrest him; but he escaped from their power.

He went back across the Jordan to the place where John first baptized, and there he remained. Many came to him and said, "John performed no sign, but everything John said about this man was true." And many there began to believe in him.

JOHN 10: 31-42

SAINT BENEDICT

"Hate no one. Do not be jealous. Do not act out of envy. . . . Pray for your enemies for the love of Christ."

RB 4.65–67, 72

REFLECTION

One of the reasons Saint Benedict's Rule has lasted through almost fifteen centuries as a guide for monastic living, and by extension to family life as well, is because Saint Benedict was not only aware of but also willing to acknowledge openly and candidly those aspects of human nature that are not very pretty or attractive: hatred, anger, jealousy, envy. He wanted his monks to confront within themselves those vices which on occasion might move them to imitate the behavior of the Jews in today's Gospel, to "pick up rocks to stone" another person rather than to imitate the compassion and forgiveness of Jesus. By exposing these vices and insisting that his monks face the sin and temptation within them, Saint Benedict was offering a means to confess and repent and be converted.

Lent confronts us in all the readings of the Masses of this season with the truth of Christ and of our all-too-human selves. Though sin and temptation and the evils of the world might dim our vision, yet does the light of Christ continue to shine brightly for those who constantly turn to him in faith.

PRAYER

Lord Jesus, strengthen us against evil and adversity, and teach us to hope. Through your grace, may we prepare ourselves well to celebrate your Resurrection and to bear witness to you each and every day. You live and reign forever and ever. Amen.

GOSPEL

Many of the Jews who had come to Mary and seen what Jesus had done began to believe in him. But some of them went to the Pharisees and told them what Jesus had done. So the chief priests and the Pharisees convened the Sanhedrin and said, "What are we going to do? This man is performing many signs. If we leave him alone, all will believe in him, and the Romans will come and take away both our land and our nation." But one of them, Caiaphas, who was high priest that year, said to them "You know nothing, nor do you consider that it is better for you that one man should die instead of the people, so that the whole nation may not perish." He did not say this on his own, but since he was high priest for that year, he prophesied that Jesus was going to die for the nation, and not only for the nation, but also to gather into one the dispersed children of God. So from that day on they planned to kill him.

So Jesus no longer walked about in public among the Jews, but he left for the region near the desert, to a town called Ephraim, and there he remained with his disciples.

Now the Passover of the Jews was near, and many went up from the country to Jerusalem before Passover to purify themselves. They looked for Jesus and said to one another as they were in the temple area, "What do you think? That he will not come to the feast?"

JOHN 11: 45-56

SAINT BENEDICT

"If it should happen that some heavy or impossible tasks are given to a brother, he should accept the order of the superior with all gentleness and obedience . . . without pride, obstinacy or refusal . . . Confident in the help of God, he must lovingly obey."

RB 68.1, 3, 5

REFLECTION

Saint Thomas Aquinas wrote of two senses of courage. There is an active courage, typical of the soldier, which enables the soldier to engage bravely in combat in defense of one's country in spite of the danger or threat to their own life. There is also a passive courage, typical of the martyr, which enables the martyr to endure patiently trials, persecution, torments, and execution. In the Gospel, the Jews look for Jesus in Jerusalem and ask one another, "What do you think? That he will not come to the feast?" How little they know of him and of his courage. Those who have followed the way of the Lord through the readings at Mass in Lent know the answer to their question: yes, he will come to the feast. Indeed, he will come to Jerusalem and he will do all that is required of him to the everlasting glory of God the Father.

Saint Benedict knew that in the monastic life there are always challenges that call for the virtue of courage, none more obvious than when a monk is asked to assume an impossible or burdensome task. All of us encounter such situations. Do we cringe in fear at tasks asked of us because we doubt our abilities or because we simply do not want to make the effort required? Are we encouraged by the example of Jesus to take courage and do our best, that in all things God may be glorified?

PRAYER

Lord God of heaven and earth, by your will all things came to be and by your will all things will return to you, the source and font of all goodness and life. May we willingly accept your grace offered to us in the sacraments and bear witness to you in a living faith, hope, and love. We ask this through Christ our Lord. Amen.

HOLY
WEEK

GOSPEL

AT THE PROCESSION WITH PALMS

When Jesus and the disciples drew near Jerusalem and came to Bethphage on the Mount of Olives, Jesus sent two disciples, saying to them, "Go into the village opposite you, and immediately you will find an ass tethered, and a colt with her. Untie them and bring them here to me. And if anyone should say anything to you, reply, 'The master has need of them.' Then he will send them at once." This happened so that what had been spoken through the prophet might be fulfilled: / *Say to daughter Zion, /"Behold, your king comes to you, / meek and riding on an ass, / and on a colt, the foal of a beast of burden."* / The disciples went and did as Jesus had ordered them. They brought the ass and the colt and laid their cloaks over them, and he sat upon them. The very large crowd spread their cloaks on the road, while others cut branches from the trees and strewed them on the road. The crowds preceding him and those following kept crying out and saying: / "Hosanna to the Son of David; / blessed is the he who comes in the name of the Lord; / hosanna in the highest." / And when he entered Jerusalem the whole city was shaken and asked, "Who is this?" And the crowds replied, "This is Jesus the prophet, from Nazareth in Galilee."

MATTHEW 21: 1-11

GOSPEL

MASS

One of the Twelve, who was called Judas Iscariot, went to the chief priests and said, "What are you willing to give me if I hand him over to you?" They paid him thirty pieces of silver, and from that time on he looked for an opportunity to hand him over.

On the first day of the Feast of Unleavened Bread, the disciples approached Jesus and said, "Where do you want us to prepare for you to eat the Passover?" He said, "Go into the city to a certain man and tell him, 'The teacher says, "My appointed time draws near; in your house I shall celebrate the Passover with my disciples."'" The disciples then did as Jesus had ordered, and prepared the Passover.

When it was evening, he reclined at table with the Twelve. And while they were eating, he said, "Amen, I say to you, one of you will betray me." Deeply distressed at this, they began to say to him one after another, "Surely it is not I, Lord?" He said in reply, "He who has dipped his hand into the dish with me is the one who will betray me. The Son of Man indeed goes, as it is written of him, but woe to that man by whom the Son of Man is betrayed. It would be better for that man if he had never been born." Then Judas, his betrayer, said in reply, "Surely it is not I, Rabbi?" He answered, "You have said so."

While they were eating, Jesus took bread, said the blessing, broke it, and giving it to his disciples said, "Take and eat; this is my body." Then he took a cup, gave thanks, and gave it to them, saying, "Drink from it, all of you, for this is my blood of the covenant, which will be shed on behalf of many for the forgiveness of sins. I tell you, from now on I shall not drink this fruit of the vine until the day when I drink it with you new in the kingdom of my Father." Then, after singing a hymn, they went out to the Mount of Olives.

Then Jesus said to them, "This night all of you will have your faith in me shaken, for it is written: / *I will strike the shepherd,* / *and the sheep* *of the flock will be dispersed;* / but after I have been raised up, I shall go before you to Galilee." Peter said to him in reply, "Though all may have their faith in you shaken, mine will never be." Jesus said to him, "Amen, I say to you, this very night before the cock crows, you will deny me three times." Peter said to him, "Even though I should have to die with you, I will not deny you." And all the disciples spoke likewise.

Then Jesus came with them to a place called Gethsemane, and he said to his disciples, "Sit here while I go over there and pray." He took along Peter and the two sons of Zebedee, and began to feel sorrow and distress. Then he said to them, "My soul is sorrowful even to death. Remain here and keep watch with me." He advanced a little and fell prostrate in prayer, saying, "My Father, if it is possible, let this cup pass from me; yet, not as I will, but as you will." When he returned to his disciples he found them asleep. He said to Peter, "So you could not keep watch with me for one hour? Watch and pray that you may not undergo the test. The spirit is willing, but the flesh is weak." Withdrawing a second time, he prayed again, "My Father, if it is not possible that this cup pass without my drinking it, your will be done!" Then he returned once more and found them asleep, for they could not keep their eyes open. He left them and withdrew again and prayed a third time, saying the same thing again. Then he returned to his disciples and said to them, "Are you still sleeping and taking your rest? Behold, the hour is at hand when the Son of Man is to be handed over to sinners. Get up, let us go. Look, my betrayer is at hand."

While he was still speaking, Judas, one of the Twelve, arrived, accompanied by a large crowd, with swords and clubs, who had come from the chief priests and the elders of the people. His betrayer had arranged a sign with them, saying, "The man I shall kiss is the one; arrest him." Immediately he went over to Jesus and said, "Hail, Rabbi!" and he kissed him. Jesus answered him, "Friend, do what you have come for." Then stepping forward they laid hands on Jesus and arrested him. And behold, one of those who accompanied Jesus put his hand to his sword, drew it, and struck the high priest's servant, cutting off his ear. Then Jesus said to him, "Put your sword back into its sheath, for all who take the sword will perish by the sword. Do you think that I cannot call upon my Father and he will not provide me at this moment with more than twelve legions of angels? But then how would the Scriptures be fulfilled which say that it must come to pass in this way?" At that hour Jesus said to the crowds, "Have you come out as against a robber, with swords and clubs to seize me? Day after day I sat teaching in the temple area, yet you did not arrest me. But all this has come to pass that the writings of the prophets may be fulfilled." Then all the disciples left him and fled.

Those who had arrested Jesus led him away to Caiaphas the high priest, where the scribes and the elders were assembled. Peter was following him at a distance as far as the high priest's courtyard, and going inside he sat down with the servants to see the outcome. The chief priests and the entire Sanhedrin kept trying to obtain false testimony against Jesus in order to put him to death, but they found none, though many false witnesses came forward. Finally two came forward who stated, "This man said, 'I can destroy the temple of God and within three days rebuild it.'" The high priest rose and addressed him, "Have you no answer? What are these men testifying against you?" But Jesus was silent. Then the high priest said to him, "I order you to tell us under oath before the living God whether you are the Christ, the Son of God." Jesus said to him in reply, "You have said so. But I tell you: / From now on you will see 'the Son of Man / seated at the right hand of the Power' / and 'coming on the clouds of heaven.'" / Then the high priest tore his robes and said, "He has blasphemed! What further need have we of witnesses? You have now heard the blasphemy; what is your opinion?" They said in reply, "He deserves to die!" Then they spat in his face and struck him, while some slapped him, saying, "Prophesy for us, Christ: who is it that struck you?"

Now Peter was sitting outside in the courtyard. One of the maids came over to him and said, "You too were with Jesus the Galilean." But he denied it in front of everyone, saying, "I do not know what you are talking about!" As he went out to the gate, another girl saw him and said to those who were there, "This man was with Jesus the Nazorean." Again he denied it with an oath, "I do not know the man!" A little later the bystanders came over and said to Peter, "Surely you too are one of them; even your speech gives you away." At that he began to curse and to swear, "I do not know the man." And immediately a cock crowed. Then Peter remembered the word that Jesus had spoken: "Before the cock crows you will deny me three times." He went out and began to weep bitterly.

When it was morning, all the chief priests and the elders of the people took counsel against Jesus to put him to death. They bound him, led him away, and handed him over to Pilate, the governor.

Then Judas, his betrayer, seeing that Jesus had been condemned, deeply regretted what he had done. He returned the thirty pieces of silver to the chief priests and elders, saying, "I have sinned in betraying innocent blood." They said, "What is that to us? Look to it yourself." Flinging the money into the temple, he departed and went off and hanged himself. The chief priests gathered up the money, but said, "It is not lawful to deposit this in the temple treasury, for it is the price of blood." After consultation, they used it to buy the potter's field as a burial place for foreigners. That is why that field even today is called the Field of Blood. Then was fulfilled what had been said through Jeremiah the prophet, / *And they took the thirty pieces of silver, / the value of a man with a price on his head, / a price set by some of the Israelites, / and they paid it out for the potter's field / just as the Lord had commanded me.*

Now Jesus stood before the governor, who questioned him, "Are you the king of the Jews?" Jesus said, "You say so." And when he was accused by the chief priests and elders, he made no answer. Then Pilate said to him, "Do you not hear how many things they are testifying against you?" But he did not answer him one word, so that the governor was greatly amazed.

Now on the occasion of the feast the governor was accustomed to release to the crowd one prisoner whom they wished. And at that time they had a notorious prisoner called Barabbas. So when they had assembled, Pilate said to them, "Which one do you want me to release to you, Barabbas, or Jesus called Christ?" For he knew that it was out of envy that they had handed him over. While he was still seated on the bench, his wife sent him a message, "Have nothing to do with that righteous man. I suffered much in a dream today because of him." The chief priests and the elders persuaded the crowds to ask for Barabbas but to destroy Jesus. The governor said to them in reply, "Which of the two do you want me to release to you?" They answered, "Barabbas!" Pilate said to them, "Then what shall I do with Jesus called Christ?" They all said, "Let him be crucified!" But he said, "Why? What evil has he done?" They only shouted the louder, "Let him be crucified!" When Pilate saw that he was not succeeding at all, but that a riot was breaking out instead, he took water and washed his hands in the sight of the crowd, saying, "I am innocent of this man's blood. Look to it yourselves." And the whole people said in reply, "His blood be upon us and upon our children." Then he released Barabbas to them, but after he had Jesus scourged, he handed him over to be crucified.

Then the soldiers of the governor took Jesus inside the praetorium and gathered the whole cohort around him. They stripped off his clothes and threw a scarlet military cloak about him. Weaving a crown out of thorns, they placed it on his head, and a reed in his right hand. And kneeling before him, they mocked him, saying, "Hail, King of the Jews!" They spat upon him and took the reed and kept striking him on the head. And when they had mocked him, they stripped him of the cloak, dressed him in his own clothes, and led him off to crucify him.

As they were going out, they met a Cyrenian named Simon; this man they pressed into service to carry his cross.

And when they came to a place called Golgotha — which means Place of the Skull —, they gave Jesus wine to drink mixed with gall. But when he had tasted it, he refused to drink. After they had crucified him, they divided his garments by casting lots; then they sat down and kept watch over him there. And they placed over his head the written charge against him: This is Jesus, the King of the Jews. Two revolutionaries were crucified with him, one on his right and the other on his left. Those passing by reviled him, shaking their heads and saying, "You who would destroy the temple and rebuild it in three days, save yourself, if you are the Son of God, and come down from the cross!" Likewise the chief priests with the scribes and elders mocked him and said, "He saved others; he cannot save himself. So he is the king of Israel! Let him come down from the cross now, and we will believe in him. He trusted in God; let him deliver him now if he wants him. For he said, 'I am the Son of God.'" The revolutionaries who were crucified with him also kept abusing him in the same way.

From noon onward, darkness came over the whole land until three in the afternoon. And about three o'clock Jesus cried out in a loud voice, *"Eli, Eli, lema sabachthani?"* which means, "My God, my God, why have you forsaken me?" Some of the bystanders who heard it said, "This one is calling for Elijah." Immediately one of them ran to get a sponge; he soaked it in wine, and putting it on a reed, gave it to him to drink. But the rest said, "Wait, let us see if Elijah comes to save him." But Jesus cried out again in a loud voice, and gave up his spirit.

Here all kneel and pause for a short time.

And behold, the veil of the sanctuary was torn in two from top to bottom. The earth quaked, rocks were split, tombs were opened, and the bodies of many saints who had fallen asleep were raised. And coming forth from their tombs after his resurrection, they entered the holy city and appeared to many. The centurion and the men with him who were keeping watch over Jesus feared greatly when they saw the earthquake and all that was happening, and they said, "Truly, this was the Son of God!" There were many women there, looking on from a distance, who had followed Jesus from Galilee, ministering to him. Among them were Mary Magdalene and Mary the mother of James and Joseph, and the mother of the sons of Zebedee.

When it was evening, there came a rich man from Arimathea named Joseph, who was himself a disciple of Jesus. He went to Pilate and asked for the body of Jesus; then Pilate ordered it to be handed over. Taking the body, Joseph wrapped it in clean linen and laid it in his new tomb that he had hewn in the rock. Then he rolled a huge stone across the entrance to the tomb and departed. But Mary Magdalene and the other Mary remained sitting there, facing the tomb.

The next day, the one following the day of preparation, the chief priests and the Pharisees gathered before Pilate and said, "Sir, we remember that this impostor while still alive said, 'After three days I will be raised up.' Give orders, then, that the grave be secured until the third day, lest his disciples come and steal him and say to the people, 'He has been raised from the dead.' This last imposture would be worse than the first." Pilate said to them, "The guard is yours; go, secure it as best you can." So they went and secured the tomb by fixing a seal to the stone and setting the guard.

MATTHEW 26: 14-75 & 27: 1-66

Shorter form: MATTHEW 27:11-54

SAINT BENEDICT

"For their part, the sick should keep in mind that they are being served out of respect for God. Therefore they should not irritate the brothers serving them with excessive demands."

RB 36.4

REFLECTION

Meekness is not always considered a virtue or strength in contemporary society for it implies a disposition to be taken advantage of by others, to allow oneself to be treated unfairly and mockingly, and all this without a murmur or whisper of complaint or protest, without the least effort to defend oneself. And yet in the Christian perspective, it is precisely the meek who will inherit the earth, who will ultimately and solely by the power of God triumph over all evil and come into the paradisiacal garden which Adam and Eve were forced to abandon in their sin. Christ is meekness personified: we are bidden to learn from him for he is "meek and humble of heart" (Mt 11:29); we are bidden to imitate him for he, Lord of all creation, entered Jerusalem "meek and riding on the colt of an ass."

While Saint Benedict does not directly speak of meekness in his Rule, it is clearly a quality he expects the monks to cultivate and practice. Those who are sick, for example, are to be meek: they are not to be demanding and complaining, but bear patiently and humbly the illnesses which they endure in order that they might be united to the sufferings of Christ. Meekness is a virtue for special reflection during Holy Week as we enter into our commemoration of those most sacred mysteries of Christ's passion, death, and Resurrection.

PRAYER

Lord God, the meekness of your son won for us eternal life. By your grace may we in turn be meek and humble of heart that our lives may reflect the radiant goodness of your son and that we may be counted among your holy ones who will inherit the earth. We make this prayer through the same Christ our Lord. Amen.

GOSPEL

PROCESSION WITH PALMS

When Jesus and his disciples drew near to Jerusalem, to Bethpage and Bethany at the Mount of Olives, he sent two of his disciples and said to them, "Go into the village opposite you, and immediately on entering it, you will find a colt tethered on which no one has ever sat. Untie it and bring it here. If anyone should say to you, 'Why are you doing this?' reply, 'The Master has need of it and will send it back here at once.'" So they went off and found a colt tethered at a gate outside on the street, and they untied it. Some of the bystanders said to them, "What are you doing, untying the colt?" They answered them just as Jesus had told them to, and they permitted them to do it. So they brought the colt to Jesus and put their cloaks over it. And he sat on it. Many people spread their cloaks on the road, and others spread leafy branches that they had cut from the fields. Those preceding him as well as those following kept crying out: / "Hosanna! / Blessed is he who comes in the name of the Lord! / Blessed is the kingdom of our father David that is to come! / Hosanna in the highest!"

MARK 11: 1-10

Alternative: JOHN 12:12-16

Gospel

Mass

The Passover and the Feast of Unleavened Bread were to take place in two days' time. So the chief priests and the scribes were seeking a way to arrest him by treachery and put him to death. They said, "Not during the festival, for fear that there may be a riot among the people."

When he was in Bethany reclining at table in the house of Simon the leper, a woman came with an alabaster jar of perfumed oil, costly genuine spikenard. She broke the alabaster jar and poured it on his head. There were some who were indignant. "Why has there been this waste of perfumed oil? It could have been sold for more than three hundred days' wages and the money given to the poor." They were infuriated with her. Jesus said, "Let her alone. Why do you make trouble for her? She has done a good thing for me. The poor you will always have with you, and whenever you wish you can do good to them, but you will not always have me. She has done what she could. She has anticipated anointing my body for burial. Amen, I say to you, wherever the gospel is proclaimed to the whole world, what she has done will be told in memory of her."

Then Judas Iscariot, one of the Twelve, went off to the chief priests to hand him over to them. When they heard him they were pleased and promised to pay him money. Then he looked for an opportunity to hand him over.

On the first day of the Feast of Unleavened Bread, when they sacrificed the Passover lamb, his disciples said to him, "Where do you want us to go and prepare for you to eat the Passover?" He sent two of his disciples and said to them, "Go into a city and a man will meet you, carrying a jar of water. Follow him. Wherever he enters, say to the master of the house, 'The Teacher says, "Where is my guest room where I may eat the Passover with my disciples?"' Then he will show you a large upper room furnished and ready. Make the preparations for us there." The disciples then went off, entered the city, and found it just as he had told them; and they prepared the Passover.

When it was evening, he came with the Twelve. And as they reclined at table and were eating, Jesus said, "Amen, I say to you, one of you will betray me, one who is eating with me." They began to be distressed and to say to him, one by one, "Surely it is not I?" He said to them, "One of the Twelve, the one who dips with me into the dish. For the Son of Man indeed goes, as it is written of him, but woe to that man by whom the Son of Man is betrayed. It would be better for that man if he had never been born."

While they were eating, he took bread, said the blessing, broke it, and gave it to them, and said, "Take it; this is my body." Then he took a cup, gave thanks, and gave it to them, and they all drank from it. He said to them, "This is my blood of the covenant, which will be shed for many. Amen, I say to you, I shall not drink again the fruit of the vine until the day when I drink it new in the kingdom of God." Then, after singing a hymn, they went out to the Mount of Olives.

Then Jesus said to them, "All of you will have your faith shaken, for it is written: / *I will strike the shepherd,* / *and the sheep will be dispersed.* / But after I have been raised up, I shall go before you to Galilee." Peter said to him, "Even though all should have their faith shaken, mine will not be." Then Jesus said to him, "Amen, I say to you, this very night before the cock crows twice you will deny me three times." But he vehemently replied, "Even though I should have to die with you, I will not deny you." And they all spoke similarly.

Then they came to a place named Gethsemane, and he said to his disciples, "Sit here while I pray." He took with him Peter, James and John, and began to be troubled and distressed. Then he said to them, "My soul is sorrowful even to death. Remain here and keep watch." He advanced a little and fell to the ground and prayed that if it were possible the hour might pass by him; he said, "Abba, Father, all things are possible to you. Take this cup away from me, but not what I will but what you will." When he returned he found them asleep. He said to Peter, "Simon, are you asleep? Could you not keep watch for one hour? Watch and pray that you may not undergo the test. The spirit is willing but the flesh is weak." Withdrawing again, he prayed, saying the same thing. Then he returned once more and found them asleep, for they could not keep their eyes open and did not know what to answer him. He returned a third time and said to them, "Are you still sleeping and taking your rest? It is enough. The hour has come. Behold, the Son of Man is to be handed over to sinners. Get up, let us go. See, my betrayer is at hand."

Then, while he was still speaking, Judas, one of the Twelve, arrived, accompanied by a crowd with swords and clubs who had come from the chief priests, the scribes, and the elders. His betrayer had arranged a signal with them, saying, "The man I shall kiss is the one; arrest him and lead him away securely." He came and immediately went over to him and said, "Rabbi." And he kissed him. At this they laid hands on him and arrested him. One of the bystanders drew his sword, struck the high priest's servant, and cut off his ear. Jesus said to them in reply, "Have you come out as against a robber, with swords and clubs, to seize me? Day after day I was with you teaching in the temple area, yet you did not arrest me; but that the Scriptures may be fulfilled." And they all left him and fled. Now a young man followed him wearing nothing but a linen cloth about his body. They seized him, but he left the cloth behind and ran off naked.

They led Jesus away to the high priest, and all the chief priests and the elders and the scribes came together. Peter followed him at a distance into the high priest's courtyard and was seated with the guards, warming himself at the fire. The chief priests and the entire Sanhedrin kept trying to obtain testimony against Jesus in order to put him to death, but they found none. Many gave false witness against him, but their testimony did not agree. Some took the stand and testified falsely against him, alleging, "We heard him say, 'I will destroy this temple made with hands and within three days I will build another not made with hands.'" Even so their testimony did not agree. The high priest rose before the assembly and questioned Jesus, saying, "Have you no answer? What are these men testifying against you?" But he was silent and answered nothing. Again the high priest asked him and said to him, "Are you the Christ, the son of the Blessed One?" Then Jesus answered, "I am; / and *you will see the Son of Man* / *seated at the right hand of the Power* / *and coming with the clouds of heaven.*" / At that the high priest tore his garments and said, "What further need have we of witnesses? You have heard the blasphemy. What do you think?" They all condemned him as deserving to die. Some began to spit on him. They blindfolded him and struck him and said to him, "Prophesy!" And the guards greeted him with blows.

While Peter was below in the courtyard, one of the high priest's maids came along. Seeing Peter warming himself, she looked intently at him and said, "You too were with the Nazarene, Jesus." But he denied it saying, "I neither know nor understand what you are talking about." So he went out into the outer court. Then the cock crowed. The maid saw him and began again to say to the bystanders, "This man is one of them." Once again he denied it. A little later the bystanders said to Peter once more, "Surely you are one of them; for you too are a Galilean." He began to curse and to swear, "I do not know this man about whom you are talking." And immediately a cock crowed a second time. Then Peter remembered the word that Jesus had said to him, "Before the cock crows twice you will deny me three times." He broke down and wept.

As soon as morning came, the chief priests with the elders and the scribes, that is, the whole Sanhedrin held a council. They bound Jesus, led him away, and handed him over to Pilate. Pilate questioned him, "Are you the king of the Jews?" He said to him in reply, "You say so." The chief priests accused him of many things. Again Pilate questioned him, "Have you no answer? See how many things they accuse you of." Jesus gave him no further answer, so that Pilate was amazed.

Now on the occasion of the feast he used to release to them one prisoner whom they requested. A man called Barabbas was then in prison along with the rebels who had committed murder in a rebellion. The crowd came forward and began to ask him to do for them as he was accustomed. Pilate answered, "Do you want me to release to you the king of the Jews?" For he knew that it was out of envy that the chief priests had handed him over. But the chief priests stirred up the crowd to have him release Barabbas for them instead. Pilate again said to them in reply, "Then what do you want me to do with the man you call the king of the Jews?" They shouted again, "Crucify him." Pilate said to them, "Why? What evil has he done?" They only shouted the louder, "Crucify him." So Pilate, wishing to satisfy the crowd, released Barabbas to them and, after he had Jesus scourged, handed him over to be crucified.

The soldiers led him away inside the palace, that is, the praetorium, and assembled the whole cohort. They clothed him in purple and, weaving a crown of thorns, placed it on him. They began to salute him with, "Hail, King of the Jews!" and kept striking his head with a reed and spitting upon him. They knelt before him in homage. And when they had mocked him, they stripped him of the purple cloak, dressed him in his own clothes, and led him out to crucify him.

They pressed into service a passer-by, Simon, a Cyrenian, who was coming in from the country, the father of Alexander and Rufus, to carry his cross. They brought him to the place of Golgotha—which is translated Place of the Skull—. They gave him wine drugged with myrrh, but he did not take it. Then they crucified him and divided his garments by casting lots for them to see what each should take. It was nine o'clock in the morning when they crucified him. The inscription of the charge against him read, "The King of the Jews." With him they crucified two revolutionaries, one on his right and one on his left. Those passing by reviled him, shaking their heads and saying, "Aha! You who would destroy the temple and rebuild it in three days, save yourself by coming down from the cross." Likewise the chief priests, with the scribes, mocked him among themselves and said, "He saved others; he cannot save himself. Let the Christ, the King of Israel, come down now from the cross that we may see and believe." Those who were crucified with him also kept abusing him. At noon darkness came over the whole land until three in the afternoon. And at three o'clock Jesus cried out in a loud voice, *"Eloi, Eloi, lema sabachthani?"* which is translated, "My God, my God, why have you forsaken me?" Some of the bystanders who heard it said, "Look, he is calling Elijah." One of them ran, soaked a sponge with wine, put it on a reed and gave it to him to drink saying, "Wait, let us see if Elijah comes to take him down." Jesus gave a loud cry and breathed his last.

Here all kneel and pause for a short time.

The veil of the sanctuary was torn in two from top to bottom. When the centurion who stood facing him saw how he breathed his last he said, "Truly this man was the Son of God!"

There were also women looking on from a distance. Among them were Mary Magdalene, Mary the mother of the younger James and of Joses, and Salome. These women had followed him when he was in Galilee and ministered to him. There were also many other women who had come up with him to Jerusalem.

When it was already evening, since it was the day of preparation, the day before the sabbath, Joseph of Arimathea, a distinguished member of the council, who was himself awaiting the kingdom of God, came and courageously went to Pilate and asked for the body of Jesus. Pilate was amazed that he was already dead. He summoned the centurion and asked him if Jesus had already died. And when he learned of it from the centurion, he gave the body to Joseph. Having bought a linen cloth, he took him down, wrapped him in the linen cloth, and laid him in a tomb that had been hewn out of the rock. Then he rolled a stone against the entrance to the tomb. Mary Magdalene and Mary the mother of Joses watched where he was laid.

MARK 14: 1-72 & 15: 1-47

Shorter form: MARK 15:1-39

SAINT BENEDICT

"When the chanter begins the Gloria, all must immediately rise from their seats out of respect and reverence for the Holy Trinity."

RB 9.7

REFLECTION

Several times a day the monks of Saint Benedict's monastery gathered for communal prayer in the oratory. Each of these hours followed a set order. Among these was the direction by Saint Benedict to stand at certain times in honor of the Holy Trinity when the words of the doxology, "Glory be to the Father and to the Son and to the Holy Spirit," were chanted. It was, in a way, the crying out of Hosanna: a joyful and exuberant recognition of the Lord's presence in their midst to sanctify their lives and their day in his service. Throughout the day the echo of all these Glorias was to inspire the monk to rededicate himself and his work and his prayer to the Lord.

Even during this special time of Holy Week, beginning today with Palm Sunday, the business of our lives and the many demands on our time can cause us to forget the glory and honor that is due to God. Let us resolve to make this week a significant one for our spiritual growth by surrounding ourselves with reminders of God's love for us. Let the palms blessed this day recall for us today and throughout the year the saving deeds of Jesus the Christ.

PRAYER

Lord Jesus Christ, you were obedient to the will of your Father and so won for us redemption. Let our gratitude express itself in words of praise and glory to you and in works of charity, kindness and forgiveness toward all. You live and reign forever and ever. Amen.

GOSPEL

PROCESSION WITH PALMS

Jesus proceeded on his journey up to Jerusalem. As he drew near to Bethpage and Bethany at the place called the Mount of Olives, he sent two of his disciples. He said, "Go into the village opposite you, and as you enter it you will find a colt tethered on which no one has ever sat. Untie it and bring it here. And if anyone should ask you, 'Why are you untying it?' you will answer, 'The Master has need of it.'" So those who had been sent went off and found everything just as he had told them. And as they were untying the colt, its owner said to them, "Why are you untying this colt?" They answered, "The Master has need of it." So they brought it to Jesus, threw their cloaks over the colt, and helped Jesus to mount. As he rode along, the people were spreading their cloaks on the road; and now as he was approaching the slope of the Mount of Olives, the whole multitude of his disciples began to praise God aloud with joy for all the mighty deeds they had seen. They proclaimed: / "Blessed is the king who comes in the name of the Lord. / Peace in heaven and glory in the highest." / Some of the Pharisees in the crowd said to him, "Teacher, rebuke your disciples." He said in reply, "I tell you, if they keep silent, the stones will cry out!"

LUKE 19: 28-40

GOSPEL

MASS

When the hour came, Jesus took his place at table with the apostles. He said to them, "I have eagerly desired to eat this Passover with you before I suffer, for, I tell you, I shall not eat it again until there is fulfillment in the kingdom of God." Then he took a cup, gave thanks, and said, "Take this and share it among yourselves; for I tell you that from this time on I shall not drink of the fruit of the vine until the kingdom of God comes." Then he took the bread, said the blessing, broke it, and gave it to them, saying, "This is my body, which will be given for you; do this in memory of me." And likewise the cup after they had eaten, saying, "This cup is the new covenant in my blood, which will be shed for you.

"And yet behold, the hand of the one who is to betray me is with me on the table; for the Son of Man indeed goes as it has been determined; but woe to that man by whom he is betrayed." And they began to debate among themselves who among them would do such a deed.

Then an argument broke out among them about which of them should be regarded as the greatest. He said to them, "The kings of the Gentiles lord it over them and those in authority over them are addressed as 'Benefactors'; but among you it shall not be so. Rather, let the greatest among you be as the youngest, and the leader as the servant. For who is greater: the one seated at table or the one who serves? Is it not the one seated at table? I am among you as the one who serves. It is you who have stood by me in my trials; and I confer a kingdom on you, just as my Father has conferred one on me, that you may eat and drink at my table in my kingdom; and you will sit on thrones judging the twelve tribes of Israel.

"Simon, Simon, behold Satan has demanded to sift all of you like wheat, but I have prayed that your own faith may not fail; and once you have turned back, you must strengthen your brothers." He said to him, "Lord, I am prepared to go to prison and to die with you." But he replied, "I tell you, Peter, before the cock crows this day, you will deny three times that you know me."

He said to them, "When I sent you forth without a money bag or a sack or sandals, were you in need of anything?" "No, nothing," they replied. He said to them, "But now one who has a money bag should take it, and likewise a sack, and one who does not have a sword should sell his cloak and buy one. For I tell you that this Scripture must be fulfilled in me, namely, *He was counted among the wicked;* and indeed what is written about me is coming to fulfillment." Then they said, "Lord, look, there are two swords here." But he replied, "It is enough!"

Then going out, he went, as was his custom, to the Mount of Olives, and the disciples followed him. When he arrived at the place he said to them, "Pray that you may not undergo the test." After withdrawing about a stone's throw from them and kneeling, he prayed, saying, "Father, if you are willing, take this cup away from me; still, not my will but yours be done." And to strengthen him an angel from heaven appeared to him. He was in such agony and he prayed so fervently that his sweat became like drops of blood falling on the ground. When he rose from prayer and returned to his disciples, he found them sleeping from grief. He said to them, "Why are you sleeping? Get up and pray that you may not undergo the test."

While he was still speaking, a crowd approached and in front was one of the Twelve, a man named Judas. He went up to Jesus to kiss him. Jesus said to him, "Judas, are you betraying the Son of Man with a kiss?" His disciples realized what was about to happen, and they asked, "Lord, shall we strike with a sword?" And one of them struck the high priest's servant and cut off his right ear. But Jesus said in reply, "Stop, no more of this!" Then he touched the servant's ear and healed him. And Jesus said to the chief priests and temple guards and elders who had come for him, "Have you come out as against a robber, with swords and clubs? Day after day I was with you in the temple area, and you did not seize me; but this is your hour, the time for the power of darkness."

After arresting him they led him away and took him into the house of the high priest; Peter was following at a distance. They lit a fire in the middle of the courtyard and sat around it, and Peter sat down with them. When a maid saw him seated in the light, she looked intently at him and said, "This man too was with him." But he denied it saying, "Woman, I do not know him." A short while later someone else saw him and said, "You too are one of them"; but Peter answered, "My friend, I am not." About an hour later, still another insisted, "Assuredly, this man too was with him, for he also is a Galilean." But Peter said, "My friend, I do not know what you are talking about." Just as he was saying this, the cock crowed, and the Lord turned and looked at Peter; and Peter remembered the word of the Lord, how he had said to him, "Before the cock crows today, you will deny me three times." He went out and began to weep bitterly. The men who held Jesus in custody were ridiculing and beating him. They blindfolded him and questioned him, saying, "Prophesy! Who is it that struck you?" And they reviled him in saying many other things against him.

When day came the council of elders of the people met, both chief priests and scribes, and they brought him before their Sanhedrin. They said, "If you are the Christ, tell us," but he replied to them, "If I tell you, you will not believe, and if I question, you will not respond. But from this time on the Son of Man will be seated at the right hand of the power of God." They all asked, "Are you then the Son of God?" He replied to them, "You say that I am." Then they said, "What further need have we for testimony? We have heard it from his own mouth."

Then the whole assembly of them arose and brought him before Pilate. They brought charges against him, saying, "We found this man misleading our people; he opposes the payment of taxes to Caesar and maintains that he is the Christ, a king." Pilate asked him, "Are you the king of the Jews?" He said to him in reply, "You say so." Pilate then addressed the chief priests and the crowds, "I find this man not guilty." But they were adamant and said, "He is inciting the people with his teaching throughout all Judea, from Galilee where he began even to here."

On hearing this Pilate asked if the man was a Galilean; and upon learning that he was under Herod's jurisdiction, he sent him to Herod, who was in Jerusalem at that time. Herod was very glad to see Jesus; he had been wanting to see him for a long time, for he had heard about him and had been hoping to see him perform some sign. He questioned him at length, but he gave him no answer. The chief priests and scribes, meanwhile, stood by accusing him harshly. Herod and his soldiers treated him contemptuously and mocked him, and after clothing him in resplendent garb, he sent him back to Pilate. Herod and Pilate became friends that very day, even though they had been enemies formerly. Pilate then summoned the chief priests, the rulers, and the people and said to them, "You brought this man to me and accused him of inciting the people to revolt. I have conducted my investigation in your presence and have not found this man guilty of the charges you have brought against him, nor did Herod, for he sent him back to us. So no capital crime has been committed by him. Therefore I shall have him flogged and then release him."

But all together they shouted out, "Away with this man! Release Barabbas to us." —Now Barabbas had been imprisoned for a rebellion that had taken place in the city and for murder.— Again Pilate addressed them, still wishing to release Jesus, but they continued their shouting, "Crucify him! Crucify him!" Pilate addressed them a third time, "What evil has this man done? I found him guilty of no capital crime. Therefore I shall have him flogged and then release him." With loud shouts, however, they persisted in calling for his crucifixion, and their voices prevailed. The verdict of Pilate was that their demand should be granted. So he released the man who had been imprisoned for rebellion and murder, for whom they asked, and he handed Jesus over to them to deal with as they wished.

As they led him away they took hold of a certain Simon, a Cyrenian, who was coming in from the country; and after laying the cross on him, they made him carry it behind Jesus. A large crowd of people followed Jesus, including many women who mourned and lamented him.

Jesus turned to them and said, "Daughters of Jerusalem, do not weep for me; weep instead for yourselves and for your children for indeed, the days are coming when people will say, 'Blessed are the barren, the wombs that never bore and the breasts that never nursed.' At that time people will say to the mountains, 'Fall upon us!' and to the hills, 'Cover us!' for if these things are done when the wood is green, what will happen when it is dry?" Now two others, both criminals, were led away with him to be executed.

When they came to the place called the Skull, they crucified him and the criminals there, one on his right, the other on his left. Then Jesus said, "Father, forgive them, they know not what they do." They divided his garments by casting lots. The people stood by and watched; the rulers, meanwhile, sneered at him and said, "He saved others, let him save himself if he is the chosen one, the Christ of God." Even the soldiers jeered at him. As they approached to offer him wine they called out, "If you are King of the Jews, save yourself." Above him there was an inscription that read, "This is the King of the Jews."

Now one of the criminals hanging there reviled Jesus, saying, "Are you not the Christ? Save yourself and us." The other, however, rebuking him, said in reply, "Have you no fear of God, for you are subject to the same condemnation? And indeed, we have been condemned justly, for the sentence we received corresponds to our crimes, but this man has done nothing criminal." Then he said, "Jesus, remember me when you come into your kingdom." He replied to him, "Amen, I say to you, today you will be with me in Paradise."

It was now about noon and darkness came over the whole land until three in the afternoon because of an eclipse of the sun. Then the veil of the temple was torn down the middle. Jesus cried out in a loud voice, "Father, into your hands I commend my spirit"; and when he had said this he breathed his last.

Here all kneel and pause for a short time.

The centurion who witnessed what had happened glorified God and said, "This man was innocent beyond doubt." When all the people who had gathered for this spectacle saw what had happened, they returned home beating their breasts; but all his acquaintances stood at a distance, including the women who had followed him from Galilee and saw these events.

Now there was a virtuous and righteous man named Joseph, who, though he was a member of the council, had not consented to their plan of action. He came from the Jewish town of Arimathea and was awaiting the kingdom of God. He went to Pilate and asked for the body of Jesus. After he had taken the body down, he wrapped it in a linen cloth and laid him in a rock-hewn tomb in which no one had yet been buried. It was the day of preparation, and the sabbath was about to begin. The women who had come from Galilee with him followed behind, and when they had seen the tomb and the way in which his body was laid in it, they returned and prepared spices and perfumed oils. Then they rested on the sabbath according to the commandment.

Luke 22: 14-71 & 23: 1-56

Shorter form: Luke 23:1-49

SAINT BENEDICT

"Whenever the brothers meet one another, the junior should ask a blessing from the senior."

RB 63.15

REFLECTION

The relations of the monks in Saint Benedict's monastery were marked in no small part by the request for and the imparting of blessings. At designated times in the Divine Office, the abbot blessed the community (RB 9.5, 11.7, 17.10). The abbot or any monk who was approached and asked for forgiveness for any offense or fault was to give a blessing to the offending but repentant monk (RB 71.8). Kitchen servers and table readers, both those beginning and those ending their week of service, were given a formal blessing (RB 35.15–18). A monk meeting a guest inside the cloister was to ask the guest for a blessing (RB 53.24). To bless someone, then, in the mind of Saint Benedict, was a sign of God's special favor and presence.

In the Gospel for today we read that the crowds in Jerusalem shouted: "Blessed is he who comes in the name of the Lord." We join our songs of praise to theirs in the celebration of the Lord's entrance into Jerusalem, but we are all too aware that the triumphal shouts of joy of this passage will soon give way to the rancorous and hateful cries of "Crucify him, crucify him!" in the Passion Narrative. We are all too aware as well that we can fail our Lord by turning from him and turning on him in so many ways. May this Holy Week truly be for us a time of blessing that we might be faithful to our Lord and his Gospel and that we might in turn bless those around us.

PRAYER

Lord Jesus, you went up to Jerusalem to endure the passion and enter into the glory of the kingdom as the firstborn of many sisters and brothers. Lead us and all your Church into the Paschal feast of everlasting life. You live and reign forever and ever. Amen.

GOSPEL

Six days before Passover Jesus came to Bethany, where Lazarus was, whom Jesus had raised from the dead. They gave a dinner for him there, and Martha served, while Lazarus was one of those reclining at table with him. Mary took a liter of costly perfumed oil made from genuine aromatic nard and anointed the feet of Jesus and dried them with her hair; the house was filled with the fragrance of the oil. Then Judas the Iscariot, one of his disciples, and the one who would betray him, said, "Why was this oil not sold for three hundred days' wages and given to the poor?" He said this not because he cared about the poor but because he was a thief and held the money bag and used to steal the contributions. So Jesus said, "Leave her alone. Let her keep this for the day of my burial. You always have the poor with you, but you do not always have me."

The large crowd of the Jews found out that he was there and came, not only because of him, but also to see Lazarus, whom he had raised from the dead. And the chief priests plotted to kill Lazarus too, because many of the Jews were turning away and believing in Jesus because of him.

JOHN 12: 1-11

SAINT BENEDICT

"One who is about to complete the week's work should do the cleaning on Saturday. They should wash the towels the brothers use to dry their hands and feet. Moreover, both the one completing service and the one beginning it should wash the feet of all."

RB 35.7–9

REFLECTION

On Saturdays, the time of preparation for the weekly celebration of the Lord's Day, those who have served in the monastery kitchen and those who are about to begin their week of service together wash the feet of all the brothers. By this act, they signify in a profound and sincere way their total commitment to serve the Lord in one another by imitating his action at the Last Supper as recorded in Saint John's Gospel (13:1–12). To do the weekly washing of feet, as well as all the towels and the utensils used in the kitchen, was not simply a hygienic exercise, but was for Saint Benedict a way of completing one's measure of service as disciples of Christ who said, "But if I wash your feet—I who am Teacher and Lord—then you must wash each other's feet" (Jn 13:14). By this washing they also show their desire to fulfill the great commandment, the *mandatum*, given at the Last Supper: "Love one another as I have loved you" (Jn 15:12).

Each day of Holy Week presents us with challenges to our faith, hope, and love. Each day we are tested to see to what extent we are willing to follow the Lord on the Way of the Cross, to see to what is the measure of service we are willing to render to all of God's people, to see how we strive to fulfill each day the new commandment of love. Lent has led us to this point in our spiritual journey. May we not turn aside from the Way to our salvation.

PRAYER

Lord Jesus, you willingly received the service of anointing at the hands of Mary as a preparation for your burial. By your grace may we serve you by our kindness and compassion to one another and so be counted among those who love you who has first loved us. You live and reign forever and ever. Amen.

GOSPEL

Reclining at table with his disciples, Jesus was deeply troubled and testified, "Amen, amen, I say to you, one of you will betray me." The disciples looked at one another, at a loss as to whom he meant. One of his disciples, the one whom Jesus loved, was reclining at Jesus' side. So Simon Peter nodded to him to find out whom he meant. He leaned back against Jesus' chest and said to him, "Master, who is it?" Jesus answered, "It is the one to whom I hand the morsel after I have dipped it." So he dipped the morsel and took it and handed it to Judas, son of Simon the Iscariot. After Judas took the morsel, Satan entered him. So Jesus said to him, "What you are going to do, do quickly." Now none of those reclining at table realized why he said this to him. Some thought that since Judas kept the money bag, Jesus had told him, "Buy what we need for the feast," or to give something to the poor. So Judas took the morsel and left at once. And it was night.

When he had left, Jesus said, "Now is the Son of Man glorified, and God is glorified in him. If God is glorified in him, God will also glorify him in himself, and he will glorify him at once. My children, I will be with you only a little while longer. You will look for me, and as I told the Jews, 'Where I go you cannot come,' so now I say it to you."

Simon Peter said to him, "Master, where are you going?" Jesus answered him, "Where I am going, you cannot follow me now, though you will follow later." Peter said to him, "Master, why can I not follow you now? I will lay down my life for you." Jesus answered, "Will you lay down your life for me? Amen, amen, I say to you, the cock will not crow before you deny me three times."

JOHN 13: 21-33, 36-38

SAINT BENEDICT

"For we are everywhere slaves of the same Lord and soldiers of the same King."

RB 61.10

REFLECTION

Today's Gospel weighs heavy with the impending darkness of the Lord's imminent arrest, trial, torture, and execution. Judas, the apostle-betrayer, possessed by the spirit of the fallen angel, departs to sell Jesus out to those who have been plotting his death. Peter, the apostle-denier, protests his willingness to die for his Lord, but in a few hours will vehemently state that he does not even know this man. The others, apostle-deserters except for the Beloved Disciple, will abandon Jesus to his fate and hide themselves away in a locked room, terrified with fear. Yet in the midst of all these human weaknesses and pathos there is glory, for the salvation of all humankind, the defeat of the Evil One, and the opening of the gates of heaven at last is at hand in the person of Jesus.

It is this King of Glory, the Redeemer and Lord of all, to whom Saint Benedict entreats his monks to offer their full loyalty, devotion, and love. From the very first verses of the Rule, Saint Benedict over and over again calls the monks to serve the Lord with uprightness, generosity, and cheerfulness. Whatever would cause a monk to betray, deny, or desert his Lord must be acknowledged and confessed so that nothing may be preferred to the love of Christ, the true King and Lord of Glory (RB 72.11 and Prol 3).

PRAYER

Lord Jesus Christ, you are the King of Glory. As the Father glorified you in your submission to his divine will for the salvation of souls, so may we, faithful to your Gospel in thought, word, and deed, come to share that same glory in the kingdom where you are Lord forever and ever. Amen.

GOSPEL

One of the Twelve, who was called Judas Iscariot, went to the chief priests and said, "What are you willing to give me if I hand him over to you?" They paid him thirty pieces of silver, and from that time on he looked for an opportunity to hand him over.

On the first day of the Feast of Unleavened Bread, the disciples approached Jesus and said, "Where do you want us to prepare for you to eat the Passover?" He said, "Go into the city to a certain man and tell him, 'The teacher says, My appointed time draws near; in your house I shall celebrate the Passover with my disciples.'" The disciples then did as Jesus had ordered, and prepared the Passover.

When it was evening, he reclined at table with the Twelve. And while they were eating, he said, "Amen, I say to you, one of you will betray me." Deeply distressed at this, they began to say to him one after another, "Surely it is not I, Lord?" He said in reply, "He who has dipped his hand into the dish with me is the one who will betray me. The Son of Man indeed goes, as it is written of him, but woe to that man by whom the Son of Man is betrayed. It would be better for that man if he had never been born." Then Judas, his betrayer, said in reply, "Surely it is not I, Rabbi?" He answered, "You have said so."

MATTHEW 26: 14-25

SAINT BENEDICT

"We must constantly recall the commandments of God, continually mulling over how hell burns the sinners who despise God, and eternal life is prepared for those who fear God."

RB 7.11

REFLECTION

In a talk given at a general audience in September of 1988, Pope John Paul II reminded those present that while the death of Jesus was attributed in Scripture to Judas, who betrayed him, to the members of the Sanhedrin, who plotted his death, and to Pilate, who gave in to the demands of the crowd out of fear, it is important to remember two crucial aspects of this event. The first is that from the cross Jesus willingly and generously forgave them all: "Father, forgive them, they do not know what they are doing" (Lk 23:24). The second is that by our own personal sin we bear responsibility as well for the crucifixion. In the words of Pope John Paul, "Through sin we have contributed to causing Christ's death for us as a victim of expiation."

On more than one occasion in the Rule, Saint Benedict reminded his monks of their obligation to live upright and sinless lives and even to remain silent when slandered or falsely accused of having committed some wrong (RB 4.30, 32). Prompted by a continual remembrance of the fear of God, that is, an awareness of the radiant and penetrating goodness of God who loves us beyond measure, the monk, and indeed every Christian, will strive to live in a way that is pleasing to God and will readily and in a spirit of love acknowledge and confess any and all sins.

PRAYER

Merciful and loving God, you call us to holiness of life in imitation of Christ, whom you sent to redeem us and who wishes to share with us the glory of his Resurrection. May we respond to your grace by witnessing the wonders of your love to all people. We make this prayer through Christ our Lord. Amen.

PASCHAL
TRIDUUM

GOSPEL

Jesus came to Nazareth, where he had grown up, and went according to his custom into the synagogue on the sabbath day. He stood up to read and was handed a scroll of the prophet Isaiah. He unrolled the scroll and found the passage where it was written:

The Spirit of the Lord is upon me,
because he has anointed me
*   to bring glad tidings to the poor.*
He has sent me to proclaim liberty to captives
*   and recovery of sight to the blind,*
*   to let the oppressed go free,*
and to proclaim a year acceptable to the Lord.

Rolling up the scroll, he handed it back to the attendant and sat down, and the eyes of all in the synagogue looked intently at him. He said to them, "Today this Scripture passage is fulfilled in your hearing."

LUKE 4: 16-21

SAINT BENEDICT

"During the days of Lent, in the morning they should be free for their readings until the end of the third hour. . . . In these Lenten days, they should each receive a separate fascicle of the Bible, which they are to read straight through to the end. These books are to be given out at the beginning of Lent."

RB 48.14–16

† The Chrism Mass is the annual Mass when the bishop blesses the oils that will be used for the sacraments throughout the year in the diocese.

REFLECTION

Saint Benedict legislated that the monks were to spend a considerable part of the day, perhaps two to four hours, doing spiritual reading or *lectio divina,* that is, a quiet and personal reading of the Scriptures. This was not a study period. Its purpose was to provide a time especially conducive to meditation, leading hopefully to contemplation. In that Saint Benedict sought to recapture some of the tradition of the early monastics of the Eastern tradition, who spent most of the day in a prayerful reading and meditation on the Scriptures. So it is not surprising during Lent not only that the time for this spiritual reading would be increased, but also that each monk would receive one of the books of the Bible for prayerful reflection during Lent. In the Scriptures the monk meets the Lord and learns to listen, deeply and openly, to the voice of the Lord calling out to the reader in order to reveal himself to him and to teach what words of the Lord were being "fulfilled in [his] hearing" that very day.

Jesus was a man of the Scriptures. When he read in the synagogue, as today's Gospel recounts, he invited those who heard him read to consider that what was said there was being fulfilled in their hearing at that moment. As we celebrate the Paschal Triduum, we need to be especially aware of the Scripture readings that give meaning to the mysteries we celebrate. The Word of God is being fulfilled in our hearing; we must attune our hearts and minds to the voice of the Lord when he speaks to us in the Scriptures.

PRAYER

Heavenly Father, at the Chrism Mass we celebrate the beginning of the ministry of the priesthood and we ask you to bless with special grace all the clergy who serve your Church. May they be the first to listen to your Word by their prayerful reading of the Scriptures and may they practice what they preach to us. May they lead us to the vision of your kingdom, where Jesus is Lord forever and ever. Amen.

GOSPEL

Before the feast of Passover, Jesus knew that his hour had come to pass from this world to the Father. He loved his own in the world and he loved them to the end. The devil had already induced Judas, son of Simon the Iscariot, to hand him over. So, during supper, fully aware that the Father had put everything into his power and that he had come from God and was returning to God, he rose from supper and took off his outer garments. He took a towel and tied it around his waist. Then he poured water into a basin and began to wash the disciples' feet and dry them with the towel around his waist. He came to Simon Peter, who said to him, "Master, are you going to wash my feet?" Jesus answered and said to him, "What I am doing, you do not understand now, but you will understand later." Peter said to him, "You will never wash my feet." Jesus answered him, "Unless I wash you, you will have no inheritance with me." Simon Peter said to him, "Master, then not only my feet, but my hands and head as well." Jesus said to him, "Whoever has bathed has no need except to have his feet washed, for he is clean all over; so you are clean, but not all." For he knew who would betray him; for this reason, he said, "Not all of you are clean."

So when he had washed their feet and put his garments back on and reclined at table again, he said to them, "Do you realize what I have done for you? You call me 'teacher' and 'master,' and rightly so, for indeed I am. If I, therefore, the master and teacher, have washed your feet, you ought to wash one another's feet. I have given you a model to follow, so that as I have done for you, you should also do."

JOHN 13: 1-15

SAINT BENEDICT

"He is to write the petition in his own hand, or certainly, if he is illiterate, he may ask someone else to write it. Then the novice makes his mark on it and personally lays it on the altar."

RB 58.20

REFLECTION

Saint Benedict spoke seldom about the celebration of Mass. In his day it was the normal practice in the Church to have Mass said only on Sunday or very special feast days. One of the instances in the Rule where he did speak of the celebration of Mass was when a novice first professed his vows. Saint Benedict said that at the time of the preparation of the gifts, having recited his vows aloud "in the presence of God and his saints" and in the presence of the abbot and monastic community, the novice then signed the written vow petition with his signature or his mark. He did this on the altar, where he left the document for the duration of the Mass. By this action he freely united the offering of his life in service to God and his brothers with the sacrifice of Christ, with the Body and Blood of his Lord which is offered to God at each Mass as a pleasing sacrifice of praise. In the reception of Holy Communion, the newly professed monk united himself more fully to Christ as he asked for the grace to be faithful to the obligations of monastic profession which he had undertaken that he might be steadfast and joyful in living out his vows and that the Lord might bring to completion the good work begun in him.

All Christians by their baptismal vows renew their oblation of themselves to the Lord each time they attend Mass and receive Holy Communion. Jesus himself taught us at the Last Supper with his disciples that the offering we make is to imitate his offering of selfless service to one another in charity and humility. As we begin this Paschal Triduum, may we be renewed in our commitment to the Lord.

PRAYER

Lord Jesus Christ, by the will of the Father and the work of the Holy Spirit, your death brought life to the world. By the sacrament of your Body and Blood, free us from all our sins, make us faithful to your Way, and never let us be separated from you. You live and reign forever and ever. Amen.*

---

*Based on the priest's prayer before receiving Holy Communion in the Roman Missal.

GOSPEL

Jesus went out with his disciples across the Kidron valley to where there was a garden, into which he and his disciples entered. Judas his betrayer also knew the place, because Jesus had often met there with his disciples. So Judas got a band of soldiers and guards from the chief priests and the Pharisees and went there with lanterns, torches, and weapons. Jesus, knowing everything that was going to happen to him, went out and said to them, "Whom are you looking for?" They answered him, "Jesus the Nazorean." He said to them, "I AM." Judas his betrayer was also with them. When he said to them, "I AM," they turned away and fell to the ground. So he again asked them, "Whom are you looking for?" They said, "Jesus the Nazorean." Jesus answered, "I told you that I AM. So if you are looking for me, let these men go." This was to fulfill what he had said, "I have not lost any of those you gave me." Then Simon Peter, who had a sword, drew it, struck the high priest's slave, and cut off his right ear. The slave's name was Malchus. Jesus said to Peter, "Put your sword into its scabbard. Shall I not drink the cup that the Father gave me?"

So the band of soldiers, the tribune, and the Jewish guards seized Jesus, bound him, and brought him to Annas first. He was the father-in-law of Caiaphas, who was high priest that year. It was Caiaphas who had counseled the Jews that it was better that one man should die rather than the people.

Simon Peter and another disciple followed Jesus. Now the other disciple was known to the high priest, and he entered the courtyard of the high priest with Jesus. But Peter stood at the gate outside. So the other disciple, the acquaintance of the high priest, went out and spoke to the gatekeeper and brought Peter in. Then the maid who was the gatekeeper said to Peter, "You are not one of this man's disciples, are you?" He said, "I am not." Now the slaves and the guards were standing around a charcoal fire that they had made, because it was cold, and were warming themselves. Peter was also standing there keeping warm.

The high priest questioned Jesus about his disciples and about his doctrine. Jesus answered him, "I have spoken publicly to the world. I have always taught in a synagogue or in the temple area where all the Jews gather, and in secret I have said nothing. Why ask me? Ask those who heard me what I said to them. They know what I said." When he had said this, one of the temple guards standing there struck Jesus and said, "Is this the way you answer the high priest?" Jesus answered him, "If I have spoken wrongly, testify to the wrong; but if I have spoken rightly, why do you strike me?" Then Annas sent him bound to Caiaphas the high priest.

Now Simon Peter was standing there keeping warm. And they said to him, "You are not one of his disciples, are you?" He denied it and said, "I am not." One of the slaves of the high priest, a relative of the one whose ear Peter had cut off, said, "Didn't I see you in the garden with him?" Again Peter denied it. And immediately the cock crowed.

Then they brought Jesus from Caiaphas to the praetorium. It was morning. And they themselves did not enter the praetorium, in order not to be defiled so that they could eat the Passover. So Pilate came out to them and said, "What charge do you bring against this man?" They answered and said to him, "If he were not a criminal, we would not have handed him over to you." At this, Pilate said to them, "Take him yourselves, and judge him according to your law." The Jews answered him, "We do not have the right to execute anyone," in order that the word of Jesus might be fulfilled that he said indicating the kind of death he would die.

So Pilate went back into the praetorium and summoned Jesus and said to him, "Are you the King of the Jews?" Jesus answered, "Do you say this on your own or have others told you about me?" Pilate answered, "I am not a Jew, am I? Your own nation and the chief priests handed you over to me. What have you done?" Jesus answered, "My kingdom does not belong to this world. If my kingdom did belong to this world, my attendants would be fighting to keep me from being handed over to the Jews. But as it is, my kingdom is not here." So Pilate said to him, "Then you are a king?" Jesus answered, "You say I am a king. For this I was born and for this I came into the world, to testify to the truth. Everyone who belongs to the truth listens to my voice." Pilate said to him, "What is truth?"

When he had said this, he again went out to the Jews and said to them, "I find no guilt in him. But you have a custom that I release one prisoner to you at Passover. Do you want me to release to you the King of the Jews?" They cried out again, "Not this one but Barabbas!" Now Barabbas was a revolutionary.

Then Pilate took Jesus and had him scourged. And the soldiers wove a crown out of thorns and placed it on his head, and clothed him in a purple cloak, and they came to him and said, "Hail, King of the Jews!" And they struck him repeatedly. Once more Pilate went out and said to them, "Look, I am bringing him out to you, so that you may know that I find no guilt in him." So Jesus came out, wearing the crown of thorns and the purple cloak. And he said to them, "Behold, the man!" When the chief priests and the guards saw him they cried out, "Crucify him, crucify him!" Pilate said to them, "Take him yourselves and crucify him. I find no guilt in him." The Jews answered, "We have a law, and according to that law he ought to die, because he made himself the Son of God." Now when Pilate heard this statement, he became even more afraid, and went back into the praetorium and said to Jesus, "Where are you from?" Jesus did not answer him. So Pilate said to him, "Do you not speak to me? Do you not know that I have power to release you and I have power to crucify you?" Jesus answered him, "You would have no power over me if it had not been given to you from above. For this reason the one who handed me over to you has the greater sin." Consequently, Pilate tried to release him;

but the Jews cried out, "If you release him, you are not a Friend of Caesar. Everyone who makes himself a king opposes Caesar."

When Pilate heard these words he brought Jesus out and seated him on the judge's bench in the place called Stone Pavement, in Hebrew, Gabbatha. It was preparation day for Passover, and it was about noon. And he said to the Jews, "Behold, your king!" They cried out, "Take him away, take him away! Crucify him!" Pilate said to them, "Shall I crucify your king?" The chief priests answered, "We have no king but Caesar." Then he handed him over to them to be crucified.

So they took Jesus, and, carrying the cross himself, he went out to what is called the Place of the Skull, in Hebrew, Golgotha. There they crucified him, and with him two others, one on either side, with Jesus in the middle. Pilate also had an inscription written and put on the cross. It read, "Jesus the Nazorean, the King of the Jews." Now many of the Jews read this inscription, because the place where Jesus was crucified was near the city; and it was written in Hebrew, Latin, and Greek. So the chief priests of the Jews said to Pilate, "Do not write 'The King of the Jews,' but that he said, 'I am the King of the Jews'." Pilate answered, "What I have written, I have written."

When the soldiers had crucified Jesus, they took his clothes and divided them into four shares, a share for each soldier. They also took his tunic, but the tunic was seamless, woven in one piece from the top down. So they said to one another, "Let's not tear it, but cast lots for it to see whose it will be," in order that the passage of Scripture might be fulfilled that says:

> They divided my garments among them,
>   and for my vesture they cast lots.

This is what the soldiers did. Standing by the cross of Jesus were his mother and his mother's sister, Mary the wife of Clopas, and Mary of Magdala. When Jesus saw his mother and the disciple there whom he loved he said to his mother, "Woman, behold, your son." Then he said to the disciple, "Behold, your mother." And from that hour the disciple took her into his home.

After this, aware that everything was now finished, in order that the Scripture might be fulfilled, Jesus said, "I thirst." There was a vessel filled with common wine. So they put a sponge soaked in wine on a sprig of hyssop and put it up to his mouth. When Jesus had taken the wine, he said, "It is finished." And bowing his head, he handed over the spirit.

Here all kneel and pause for a short time.

Now since it was preparation day, in order that the bodies might not remain on the cross on the sabbath, for the sabbath day of that week was a solemn one, the Jews asked Pilate that their legs be broken and that they be taken down. So the soldiers came and broke the legs of the first and then of the other one who was crucified with Jesus. But when they came to Jesus and saw that he was already dead, they did not break his legs, but one soldier thrust his lance into his side, and immediately blood and water flowed out. An eyewitness has testified, and his testimony is true; he knows that he is speaking the truth, so that you also may come to believe. For this happened so that the Scripture passage might be fulfilled: *Not a bone of it will be broken.* And again another passage says: *They will look upon him whom they have pierced.*

After this, Joseph of Arimathea, secretly a disciple of Jesus for fear of the Jews, asked Pilate if he could remove the body of Jesus. And Pilate permitted it. So he came and took his body. Nicodemus, the one who had first come to him at night, also came bringing a mixture of myrrh and aloes weighing about one hundred pounds. They took the body of Jesus and bound it with burial cloths along with the spices, according to the Jewish burial custom. Now in the place where he had been crucified there was a garden, and in the garden a new tomb, in which no one had yet been buried. So they laid Jesus there because of the Jewish preparation day; for the tomb was close by.

JOHN 18: 1-40 & 19: 1-42

SAINT BENEDICT

"Then we will never depart from his teaching and we will persevere in his doctrine in the monastery until death. Likewise, we will participate in the passion of Christ through patience so as to deserve to be companions in his kingdom. Amen."

RB PROLOGUE 50

REFLECTION

When all is said and done, it is the gift of perseverance in the monastery unto death that for Saint Benedict marks a monk's commitment to his vows. Whatever may be the physical, psychological, or spiritual infirmities, be they few or many, from which he might suffer, it is indeed a great miracle and sign of God's grace and love that the monk remains true until death to the vows he made on the day of his profession. Not knowing what the future would hold but willing to submit his will to the will of the Father as manifested in the person of the abbot and in the brothers of his community, the monk put his faith in God and promised to seek God with a firmness of purpose and resolve. It is as the vows professed at a wedding ceremony demand: for better, for worse, for richer, for poorer, in sickness, in health until death.

In Saint John's account of the Passion, the last words of Jesus on the cross are: "It is finished." All who call themselves Christians are called to make this same testimony, whether they have professed religious vows or marriage vows or live in the world as singles: all have a calling and a commitment as baptized Christians to follow the way of Christ in their daily lives, to ask for God's help in being faithful to the end, and to intercede for and assist others in their journeys to the kingdom of heaven. May the words of Jesus, "It is finished," be our words at the end of each day as we offer that day to the Father as a sacrifice of praise and thanksgiving for the love with which he has loved us.

PRAYER

Lord Jesus Christ, you willingly handed yourself over to death for our salvation. Grant that we may persevere in our Christian vocation and be steadfast in faith, hope, and love, so that we may follow the narrow way that leads to eternal life. You live and reign forever and ever. Amen.

GOSPEL

After the sabbath, as the first day of the week was dawning, Mary Magdalene and the other Mary came to see the tomb. And behold, there was a great earthquake; for an angel of the Lord descended from heaven, approached, rolled back the stone, and sat upon it. His appearance was like lightning and his clothing was white as snow. The guards were shaken with fear of him and became like dead men. Then the angel said to the women in reply, "Do not be afraid! I know that you are seeking Jesus the crucified. He is not here, for he has been raised just as he said. Come and see the place where he lay. Then go quickly and tell his disciples, 'He has been raised from the dead, and he is going before you to Galilee; there you will see him.' Behold, I have told you." Then they went away quickly from the tomb, fearful yet overjoyed, and ran to announce this to his disciples. And behold, Jesus met them on their way and greeted them. They approached, embraced his feet, and did him homage. Then Jesus said to them, "Do not be afraid. Go tell my brothers to go to Galilee, and there they will see me."

MATTHEW 28: 1-10

SAINT BENEDICT

"I will sing to you in the presence of the angels. *So let us be careful how we believe in the sight of God and his angels. And let us stand to sing in such a way that our mind is in harmony with our voice.*"

RB 19.5–7

REFLECTION

It is clear from a careful reading of his Rule that Saint Benedict was no romantic. He was firmly grounded in his understanding of human nature and its foibles, and he was fully aware of the failings to which even monks are prone. He was also firmly grounded in his belief in the abiding presence of God. It was this belief that affirmed for him also the abiding and providential presence of the angels, the divine messengers of God who worship before the throne of God and sing his everlasting praises. These blessed spirits, he held, were especially present when the Divine Office was sung and the monks were reminded that such a holy company ought to encourage them to be especially attentive to what they pray and how they pray. The companionship, and indeed the friendship, of these powerful agents of God was a kind of miracle, a blessing for the community.

In our contemporary sophistication, we seldom consider the angels. Yet the Scriptures are clear. In the Gospel for today, it was an angel of the Lord who came to earth on Easter morning. His appearance caused an earthquake as he rolled back the stone that covered the entrance to the burial cave where the body of Jesus had been laid and then sat on the stone. "His appearance was like lightening and his clothing was white as snow" and yet he spoke with gentleness to the women, announcing the Resurrection. May the angels of God continue to be present to us today and every day, that we might sing the praises of the Lord in their company as they announce the Good News of salvation.

PRAYER

Lord Jesus Christ, through the message of an angel, Mary learned of your coming as man and through the message of an angel your glorious Resurrection was first revealed to the women. May we be blessed by the glorious company of angels as we strive to live your Word and may we sing your praises with them forever in heaven, where you live and reign world without end. Amen.

GOSPEL

When the sabbath was over, Mary Magdalene, Mary, the mother of James, and Salome bought spices so that they might go and anoint him. Very early when the sun had risen, on the first day of the week, they came to the tomb. They were saying to one another, "Who will roll back the stone for us from the entrance to the tomb?" When they looked up, they saw that the stone had been rolled back; it was very large. On entering the tomb they saw a young man sitting on the right side, clothed in a white robe, and they were utterly amazed. He said to them, "Do not be amazed! You seek Jesus of Nazareth, the crucified. He has been raised; he is not here. Behold the place where they laid him. "But go and tell his disciples and Peter, 'He is going before you to Galilee; there you will see him, as he told you.'"

MARK 16: 1-7

SAINT BENEDICT

"The fear of the Lord keeps these people from vaunting themselves for their good performance, for they know that what is good in themselves could not have come about except for the Lord. They heap praise on the Lord working in them, saying with the prophet: 'Not to us, Lord, not to us, but to your name give the glory.'"

RB PROLOGUE 29–30

REFLECTION

When the women arrive at the tomb, they are amazed to see a young man, "sitting on the right side, clothed in a white robe." He announces the resurrection of Jesus and bids the women to go and tell the disciples and Peter to meet Jesus in Galilee, as Jesus had instructed them. There they will see him. In this account the evangelist Mark captures the quiet and still yet almighty and divine power and force at work in the resurrection. The women, though amazed, are not terrified or scared to death. There is something about the young man that moves them deeply to believe him and to trust that his words are true.

Saint Benedict was very much aware of the divine power working in the lives of people. All that is good is the result of this power and all praise is to be given to God, many times a day, for the goodness with which we have been blessed. But even more, Saint Benedict wanted his monks to enter into the stillness and calm of that divine power, an entry available to them, he thought and taught, only through the silence and tranquility of common prayer, spiritual reading, and an attitude of recollection, of awareness throughout the day of the presence of God. That power raised Jesus from the dead. That same power can free us from sin, help us to overcome temptation, respond with kindness and forgiveness to all who trouble us, and embrace all, even our enemies, with the sign of peace.

PRAYER

Lord God of heaven and earth, the Resurrection of your Son Jesus Christ brought new life to the world. May we who celebrate the glory of this day be filled with joy and yearn for the fullness of that redemption in the kingdom of heaven, where Jesus is Lord forever and ever. Amen.

GOSPEL

At daybreak on the first day of the week the women who had come from Galilee with Jesus took the spices they had prepared and went to the tomb. They found the stone rolled away from the tomb; but when they entered, they did not find the body of the Lord Jesus. While they were puzzling over this, behold, two men in dazzling garments appeared to them. They were terrified and bowed their faces to the ground. They said to them, "Why do you seek the living one among the dead? He is not here, but he has been raised. Remember what he said to you while he was still in Galilee, that the Son of Man must be handed over to sinners and be crucified, and rise on the third day." And they remembered his words. Then they returned from the tomb and announced all these things to the eleven and to all others. The women were Mary Magdalene, Joanna, and Mary the mother of James; the others who accompanied them also told this to the apostles, but their story seemed like nonsense and they did not believe them. But Peter got up and ran to the tomb, bent down, and saw the burial cloths alone; then he went home amazed at what had happened.

LUKE 24: 1-12

SAINT BENEDICT

"From Holy Easter until Pentecost, Alleluia is sung without exception in both psalms and responsories."

RB 15.1

REFLECTION

The account of the finding of the empty tomb in the Gospel of Luke begins: "At daybreak on the first day of the week . . ." This is the time of day, the rising of the sun, for the monastic celebration of the Divine Office for Lauds, the great prayer of praise. At Lauds the community greets the Dawn from on high, the Radiant Sun who gives us light and peace and joy to all the world. Having spent some time in Vigil in the darkness awaiting the coming of the light, the community now greets the day with hymns and psalms of joyful praise. This is especially the case on Sunday morning, "the first day of the week," which commemorates in a special way the Lord's Resurrection. It is especially the case on Easter Sunday, for it is on that day and for the next fifty days until the feast of Pentecost that the celebration of Lauds is filled with "Alleluias" from beginning to end, and the community prays as one that the power of the Resurrection will fill their lives with grace and light that they might faithfully fulfill their obligations as Christians and as monks.

The forty days of Lent and the celebration of the Triduum have come to an end. We bask in the glory of this Easter Vigil: the Service of the Light with the blessing of the fire and the lighting of the Paschal Candle, which symbolizes for us the Light of Christ; the Liturgy of the Word with those beautiful readings of the Scriptures that recall our salvation; the Liturgy of Baptism with the blessing and sprinkling of the water to remind us of our baptism; the celebration of the Eucharist and the reception of the very Body and Blood of the Lord given for us. May the Easter Alleluia never fade in our hearts.

PRAYER

Lord Jesus Christ, you have won for us eternal salvation by your passion, death, and Resurrection. May we who walk in your light be witnesses to your truth and your way, you who have turned our mourning into joy. You are Lord forever and ever. Amen.

EASTER
SUNDAY

GOSPEL

On the first day of the week, Mary of Magdala came to the tomb early in the morning, while it was still dark, and saw the stone removed from the tomb. So she ran and went to Simon Peter and to the other disciple whom Jesus loved, and told them, "They have taken the Lord from the tomb, and we don't know where they put him." So Peter and the other disciple went out and came to the tomb. They both ran, but the other disciple ran faster than Peter and arrived at the tomb first; he bent down and saw the burial cloths there, but did not go in. When Simon Peter arrived after him, he went into the tomb and saw the burial cloths there, and the cloth that had covered his head, not with the burial cloths but rolled up in a separate place. Then the other disciple also went in, the one who had arrived at the tomb first, and he saw and believed. For they did not yet understand the Scripture that he had to rise from the dead.

JOHN 20: 1-9

Alternative readings from Easter Vigil or LUKE 24:13-35
at an afternoon or evening Mass.

SAINT BENEDICT

"Let him deny his body some food, some drink, some sleep, some chatter, some joking, and let him await Holy Easter with the joy of spiritual desire."

RB 49.7

REFLECTION

On Ash Wednesday, we reflected that for Saint Benedict the life of the monk ought to have about it at all times and in all seasons the character of a Lenten observance. This is a call to a life of discipline and a willingness to deny oneself some of the "pleasures" of life. But it was not Saint Benedict's intention to suggest that penance and atonement ought to be the sole or even the primary concerns of a monk's life. Rather the practices of Lent were seen by him to be the best ways for the monk to prepare himself for the wonder of Easter that will be fulfilled in him when the time of his earthly life has come to an end and by the grace and mercy of God he, faithful to his calling and persevering in the monastery until death, may find welcome in the kingdom of heaven. It is the "joy of spiritual desire" that Saint Benedict wishes to instill in his disciples that they might live now in anticipation of the life to come and union with the God whom they have sought from the moment of their first profession.

All Christians are destined for the glorious life of the kingdom of God won for us by Christ. With the Psalmist we say, "Happy are those whose strength you are, their hearts are set upon the pilgrimage." The feast of Easter reminds us that the promise that Jesus made to his disciples and to us to bring us to everlasting life will be fulfilled. May that promise guide us in our choices each day of our lives.

PRAYER

Heavenly Father, we are filled with joy and our hearts and voices resound with Alleluias as we celebrate the splendor of the day of Resurrection of your only begotten Son. His light illumines all creation with the glory of your love. May we be loving disciples of your Son who shares his life with us and so be blessed with the vision of you in the life to come. We ask this through Christ our Risen Lord. Amen.

APPENDIX A:
CALENDAR OF LENT 2010-2019
& LECTIONARY CYCLE

Ash Wednesday–Easter

Year	Sunday Year	Lent	Date
2010	C	Ash Wednesday	February 17
		1st Sunday of Lent	February 21
		2nd Sunday of Lent	February 28
		3rd Sunday of Lent	March 7
		4th Sunday of Lent	March 14
		5th Sunday of Lent	March 21
		Palm Sunday	March 28
		Paschal Triduum	April 1
		Easter Sunday	April 4
2011	A	Ash Wednesday	March 9
		1st Sunday of Lent	March 13
		2nd Sunday of Lent	March 20
		3rd Sunday of Lent	March 27
		4th Sunday of Lent	April 3
		5th Sunday of Lent	April 10
		Palm Sunday	April 17
		Paschal Triduum	April 21
		Easter Sunday	April 24

Year	Sunday Year	Lent	Date
2012	B	Ash Wednesday	February 22
		1st Sunday of Lent	February 26
		2nd Sunday of Lent	March 4
		3rd Sunday of Lent	March 11
		4th Sunday of Lent	March 18
		5th Sunday of Lent	March 25
		Palm Sunday	April 1
		Paschal Triduum	April 5
		Easter Sunday	April 8
2013	C	Ash Wednesday	February 13
		1st Sunday of Lent	February 17
		2nd Sunday of Lent	February 24
		3rd Sunday of Lent	March 3
		4th Sunday of Lent	March 10
		5th Sunday of Lent	March 17
		Palm Sunday	March 24
		Paschal Triduum	March 28
		Easter Sunday	March 31

Year	Sunday Year	Lent	Date
2014	A	Ash Wednesday	March 5
		1st Sunday of Lent	March 9
		2nd Sunday of Lent	March 16
		3rd Sunday of Lent	March 23
		4th Sunday of Lent	March 30
		5th Sunday of Lent	April 6
		Palm Sunday	April 13
		Paschal Triduum	April 17
		Easter Sunday	April 20
2015	B	Ash Wednesday	February 18
		1st Sunday of Lent	February 22
		2nd Sunday of Lent	March 1
		3rd Sunday of Lent	March 8
		4th Sunday of Lent	March 15
		5th Sunday of Lent	March 22
		Palm Sunday	March 29
		Paschal Triduum	April 2
		Easter Sunday	April 5

Year	Sunday Year	Lent	Date
2016	C	Ash Wednesday	February 10
		1st Sunday of Lent	February 14
		2nd Sunday of Lent	February 21
		3rd Sunday of Lent	February 28
		4th Sunday of Lent	March 6
		5th Sunday of Lent	March 13
		Palm Sunday	March 20
		Paschal Triduum	March 24
		Easter Sunday	March 27
2017	A	Ash Wednesday	March 1
		1st Sunday of Lent	March 5
		2nd Sunday of Lent	March 12
		3rd Sunday of Lent	March 19
		4th Sunday of Lent	March 26
		5th Sunday of Lent	April 2
		Palm Sunday	April 9
		Paschal Triduum	April 13
		Easter Sunday	April 16

Year	Sunday Year	Lent	Date
2018	B	Ash Wednesday	February 14
		1st Sunday of Lent	February 18
		2nd Sunday of Lent	February 25
		3rd Sunday of Lent	March 4
		4th Sunday of Lent	March 11
		5th Sunday of Lent	March 18
		Palm Sunday	March 25
		Paschal Triduum	March 29
		Easter Sunday	April 1
2019	C	Ash Wednesday	March 6
		1st Sunday of Lent	March 10
		2nd Sunday of Lent	March 17
		3rd Sunday of Lent	March 24
		4th Sunday of Lent	March 31
		5th Sunday of Lent	April 7
		Palm Sunday	April 14
		Paschal Triduum	April 18
		Easter Sunday	April 21

APPENDIX B:
SELECTIONS FROM THE
RULE OF SAINT BENEDICT

Ash Wednesday	49.2–3
Thursday	Prologue 2–3
Friday	41.7
Saturday	Prologue 1
1st Sunday A	Prologue 28
1st Sunday B	5.1–2
1st Sunday C	5.12ab, 13
Monday 1	36.1–3 and 53.1
Tuesday 1	13.12–13
Wednesday 1	2.2–3
Thursday 1	20.1–3
Friday 1	4.3
Saturday 1	7.67
2nd Sunday A	58.6–8
2nd Sunday B	58.1–4a
2nd Sunday C	6.6
Monday 2	64.9b–11
Tuesday 2	7.68–70
Wednesday 2	66.1, 3–4
Thursday 2	31.9a
Friday 2	7.34
Saturday 2	27.5–6
3rd Sunday A	72.8–12
3rd Sunday B	52.1–2, 4
3rd Sunday C	25.1–3a
Monday 3	73.8–9
Tuesday 3	46.5–6
Wednesday 3	18.2–3, 7–8, 11
Thursday 3	7.35–36
Friday 3	4.1–2
Saturday 3	7.64–65
4th Sunday A	Prologue 9a
4th Sunday B	4.28
4th Sunday C	27.5

Monday 4	20.4a
Tuesday 4	Prologue 19–20
Wednesday 4	5.10–11
Thursday 4	Prologue 14–15
Friday 4	4.44–45
Saturday 4	4.78
5th Sunday A	4.41
5th Sunday B	5.3–4
5th Sunday C	7.51
Monday 5 Years A and B	4.25
Monday Year C	8.4
Tuesday 5	7.8–9
Wednesday 5	Prologue 2
Thursday 5	Prologue 42–44
Friday 5	4.65–67, 72
Saturday 5	68.1, 3, 5
Passion Sunday A	36.4
Passion Sunday B	9.7
Passion Sunday C	63.15
Monday of Holy Week	35.7–9
Tuesday of Holy Week	61.10
Wednesday of Holy Week	7.11
Chrism Mass	48.14–16
Holy Thursday	58.20
Good Friday	Prologue 50
Holy Saturday-Vigil Mass A	19.5–7
Holy Saturday-Vigil Mass B	Prologue 29–30
Holy Saturday-Vigil Mass C	15.1
Easter Sunday	49.7

SUGGESTIONS FOR FURTHER READING

SAINT BENEDICT, HIS LIFE, AND HIS RULE

Doyle, Leonard J., trans. *The Rule of Saint Benedict.* Collegeville, MN: The Liturgical Press, 2001.

Fry, Timothy, O.S.B., ed. *RB 1980: The Rule of St. Benedict.* Collegeville, MN: The Liturgical Press, 1981.

Saint Gregory the Great. *The Life of Saint Benedict.* Translated by Hilary Costello and Eoin de Bhaldraithe with commentary by Adalbert de Vogüé, O.S.B. Petersham, MA: St. Bede's Publications, 1993.

Kardong, Terrence. *Benedict's Rule: A Translation and Commentary.* Collegeville, MN: The Liturgical Press, 1996. The translation used in this book.

BENEDICTINE SPIRITUALITY FOR TODAY

Canham, Elizabeth J. *Heart Whispers: Benedictine Wisdom for Today.* Nashville, TN: Upper Room Books, 1999.

de Waal, Esther. *Living with Contradiction: Reflections on the Rule of St. Benedict.* San Francisco: Harper & Row, 1989.

———. *Seeking God: The Way of St. Benedict.* Collegeville, MN: The Liturgical Press, 1984.

Dollard, Kit, et al. *Doing Business with Benedict, The Rule of St. Benedict and Business Management: A Conversation.* London: Continuum, 2002.

Galbraith, Craig S., and Oliver Galbraith, III. *The Benedictine Rule of Leadership: Classic Management Secrets You Can Use Today.* Avon, MA: Adams Media, 2004.

Grün, Anselm, O.S.B. *Benedict of Nursia: His Message for Today.* Collegeville, MN: The Liturgical Press, 2006.

Homan, Daniel, O.S.B., and Lonni Collins Pratt. *Radical Hospitality: Benedict's Way of Love.* Brewster, MA: Paraclete Press, 2002.

Longenecker, Dwight. *Listen My Son: Saint Benedict for Fathers.* Harrisburg, PA: Morehouse, 1999.

Merret-Crosby, Anthony, ed. *The Benedictine Handbook.* Collegeville, MN: The Liturgical Press, 2003.

Norris, Kathleen. *A Cloister Walk.* New York: Riverhead Books, 1996.

Robinson, David. *The Family Cloister: Benedictine Wisdom for the Home.* New York: Crossroads, 2000.

Swan, Laura. *Engaging Benedict: What the Rule Can Teach Us Today.* Notre Dame, IN: Ave Maria Press, 2005.

Tvedten, Benet. *How to Be a Monastic and Not Leave Your Day Job.* Brewster, MA: Paraclete Press, 2006.

Wilkes, Paul. *Beyond the Walls: Monastic Wisdom for Everyday Life.* New York: Doubleday, 1999.

INTERNET
RESOURCES

The Order of Saint Benedict Web site available at
http://www.osb.org

Saint Anselm Abbey Web site available at
http://www.anselm.edu/administration/the+abbey/

Saint Anselm College Web site available at
http://www.anselm.edu

Christus Publishing, LLC Web site available at
http://www.christuspublishing.com

COVER ART

The front cover is adorned with a detail section depicting Saint Benedict that is within a larger fresco of the Crucifixion of Jesus Christ by Fra Angelico (1395–1455) located in the Convento di San Marco, Florence, Italy.

ABOUT THE AUTHOR

Fr. John R. Fortin, O.S.B., has been a Benedictine monk at Saint Anselm Abbey in Manchester, NH, since 1970. He earned a bachelor's degree in philosophy from Saint Anselm College in 1972. After completing theological studies at St. John's Seminary in Brighton, MA, he was ordained to the priesthood in 1976. He obtained a master's degree in liberal arts education from St. John's College in Santa Fe, NM, in 1979 and a master's degree (1984) and doctorate (1992) in medieval studies from the University of Notre Dame's Medieval Institute.

He taught and was headmaster at Woodside Priory School, a college preparatory school in Portola Valley, CA, from 1976–1981. He has served in many capacities at Saint Anselm College, including Dean of Students, a member of the Governing Board, and a member of the Faculty Senate. He is currently a professor in the Philosophy Department. He has served on and chaired the Advisory Board of Trinity High School, a Catholic school in Manchester, NH, and on the Diocesan School Board. He has served two terms on the Presbyteral Council of the Diocese of Manchester.

He has published articles on Saint Augustine, Boethius, Saint Benedict, Saint Anselm, and other medieval figures in such journals as *The American Catholic Philosophical Quarterly, The American Benedictine Review, The Downside Review, The International Philosophical Quarterly, Cistercian Studies Quarterly, The Journal of Early Christian Studies,* and *The Modern Schoolman.* He has authored, edited, and/or contributed to several books. In 2001 he founded the Institute for Saint Anselm Studies and was its director for six years. In 2007–2008, he was a Visiting Scholar at the Jacques Maritain Center, University of Notre Dame.

green press
INITIATIVE

Christus Publishing, LLC is committed to preserving ancient forests and natural resources. We elected to print this title on 30% postconsumer recycled paper, processed chlorine-free. As a result, we have saved:

7 Trees (40' tall and 6-8" diameter)
2 Million BTUs of Total Energy
660 Pounds of Greenhouse Gases
3,179 Gallons of Wastewater
193 Pounds of Solid Waste

Christus Publishing, LLC made this paper choice because our printer, Thomson-Shore, Inc., is a member of Green Press Initiative, a nonprofit program dedicated to supporting authors, publishers, and suppliers in their efforts to reduce their use of fiber obtained from endangered forests.

For more information, visit www.greenpressinitiative.org

Environmental impact estimates were made using the Environmental Defense Paper Calculator. For more information visit: www.edf.org/papercalculator